AF322669

WORD PROBLEMS ARE EASY!

Math Books for 1st Graders
Children's Math Books

HI KIDS!
Help us solve these easy addition word problems.

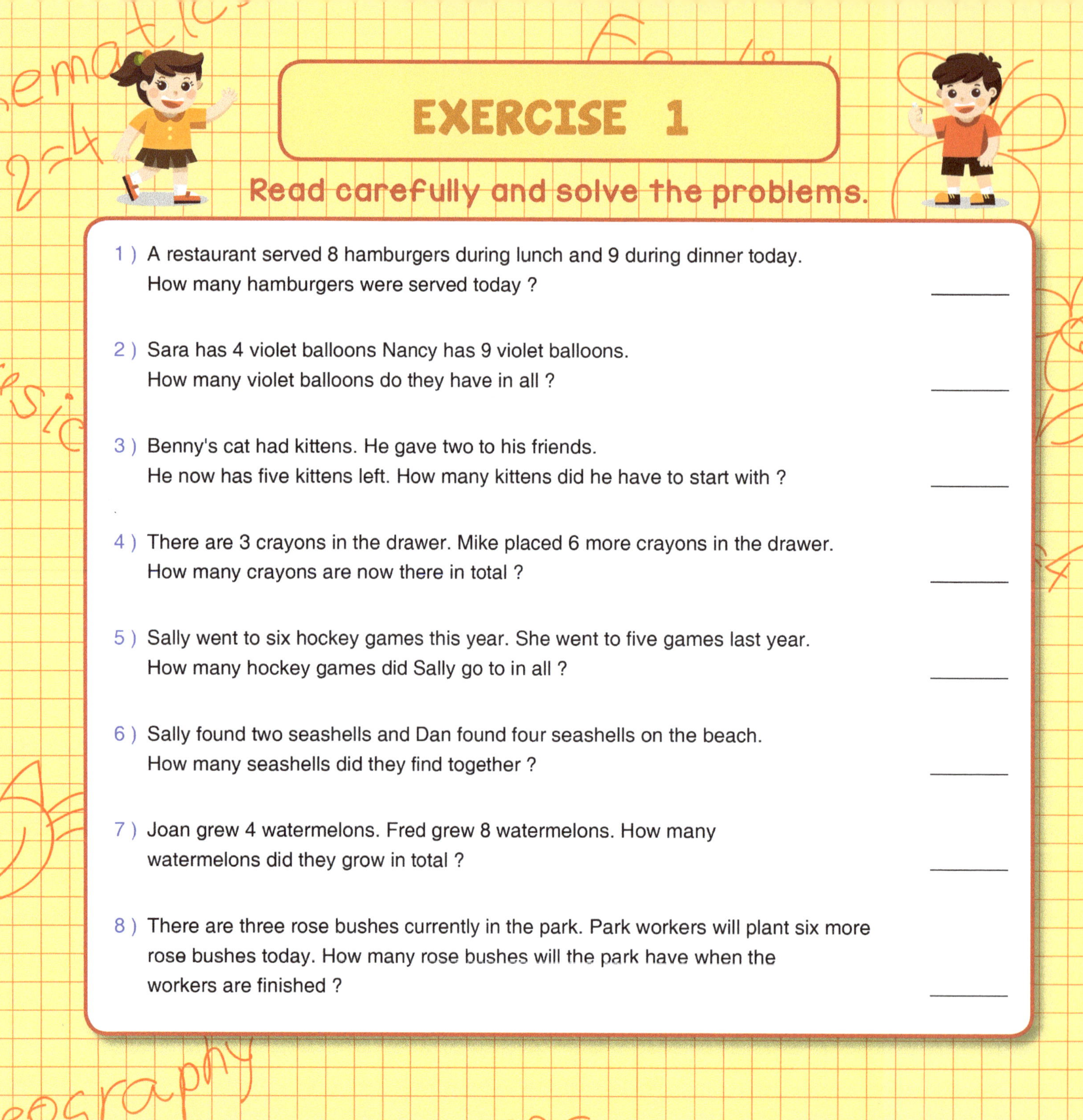

EXERCISE 1

Read carefully and solve the problems.

1) A restaurant served 8 hamburgers during lunch and 9 during dinner today.
How many hamburgers were served today ? ________

2) Sara has 4 violet balloons Nancy has 9 violet balloons.
How many violet balloons do they have in all ? ________

3) Benny's cat had kittens. He gave two to his friends.
He now has five kittens left. How many kittens did he have to start with ? ________

4) There are 3 crayons in the drawer. Mike placed 6 more crayons in the drawer.
How many crayons are now there in total ? ________

5) Sally went to six hockey games this year. She went to five games last year.
How many hockey games did Sally go to in all ? ________

6) Sally found two seashells and Dan found four seashells on the beach.
How many seashells did they find together ? ________

7) Joan grew 4 watermelons. Fred grew 8 watermelons. How many
watermelons did they grow in total ? ________

8) There are three rose bushes currently in the park. Park workers will plant six more
rose bushes today. How many rose bushes will the park have when the
workers are finished ? ________

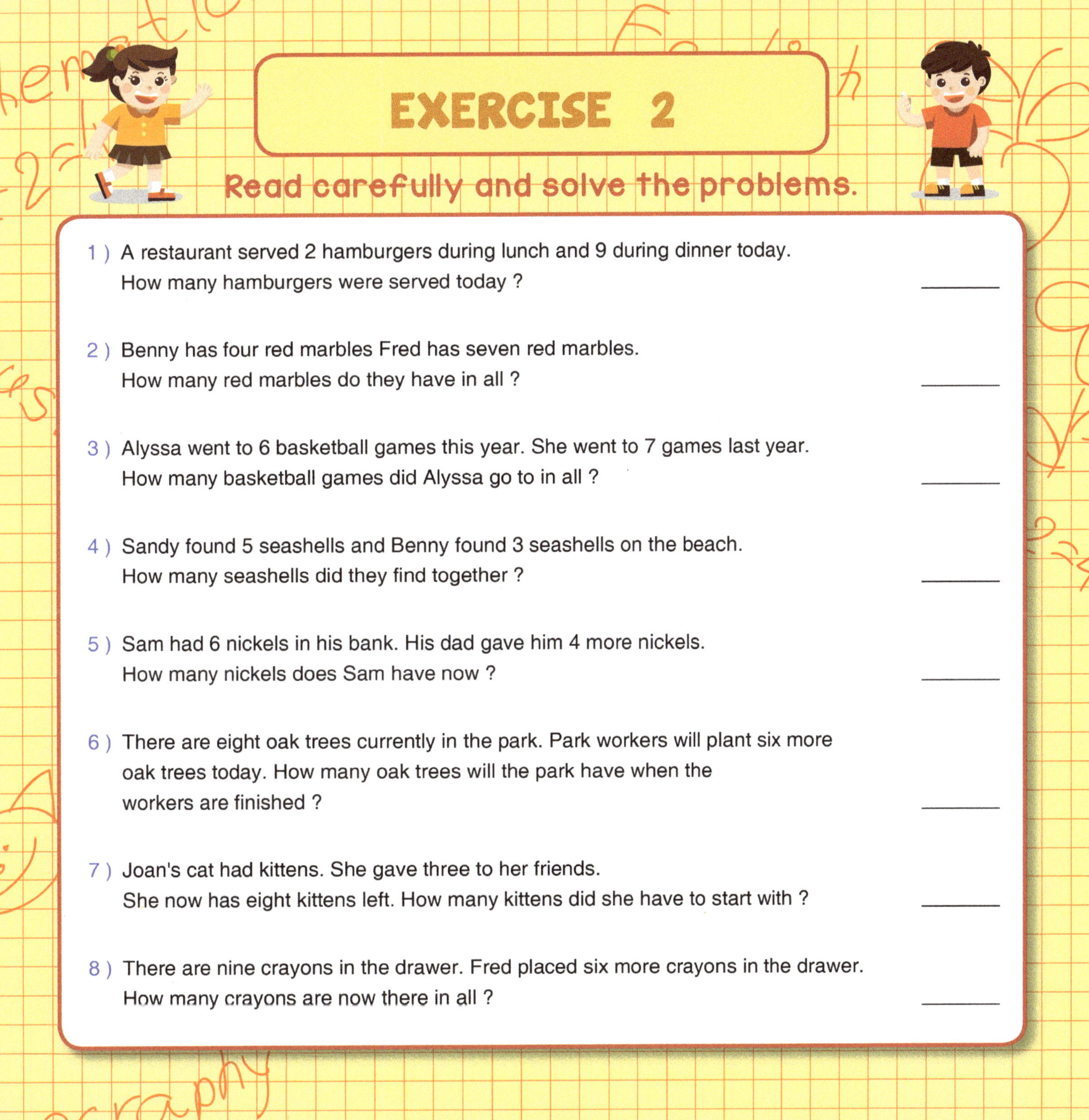

EXERCISE 2

Read carefully and solve the problems.

1) A restaurant served 2 hamburgers during lunch and 9 during dinner today.
How many hamburgers were served today ?   _______

2) Benny has four red marbles Fred has seven red marbles.
How many red marbles do they have in all ?   _______

3) Alyssa went to 6 basketball games this year. She went to 7 games last year.
How many basketball games did Alyssa go to in all ?   _______

4) Sandy found 5 seashells and Benny found 3 seashells on the beach.
How many seashells did they find together ?   _______

5) Sam had 6 nickels in his bank. His dad gave him 4 more nickels.
How many nickels does Sam have now ?   _______

6) There are eight oak trees currently in the park. Park workers will plant six more
oak trees today. How many oak trees will the park have when the
workers are finished ?   _______

7) Joan's cat had kittens. She gave three to her friends.
She now has eight kittens left. How many kittens did she have to start with ?   _______

8) There are nine crayons in the drawer. Fred placed six more crayons in the drawer.
How many crayons are now there in all ?   _______

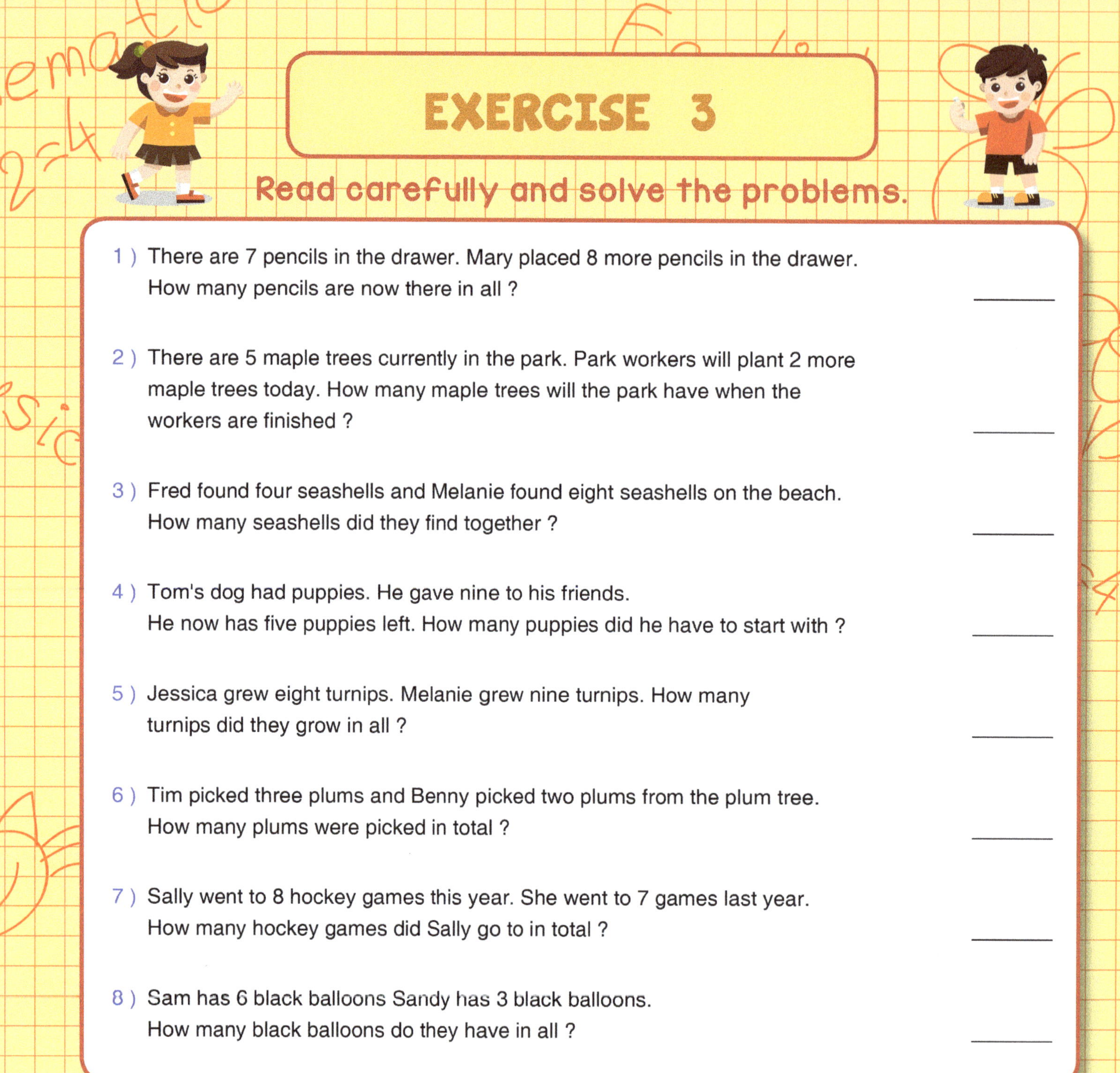

EXERCISE 3

Read carefully and solve the problems.

1) There are 7 pencils in the drawer. Mary placed 8 more pencils in the drawer. How many pencils are now there in all ? ______

2) There are 5 maple trees currently in the park. Park workers will plant 2 more maple trees today. How many maple trees will the park have when the workers are finished ? ______

3) Fred found four seashells and Melanie found eight seashells on the beach. How many seashells did they find together ? ______

4) Tom's dog had puppies. He gave nine to his friends. He now has five puppies left. How many puppies did he have to start with ? ______

5) Jessica grew eight turnips. Melanie grew nine turnips. How many turnips did they grow in all ? ______

6) Tim picked three plums and Benny picked two plums from the plum tree. How many plums were picked in total ? ______

7) Sally went to 8 hockey games this year. She went to 7 games last year. How many hockey games did Sally go to in total ? ______

8) Sam has 6 black balloons Sandy has 3 black balloons. How many black balloons do they have in all ? ______

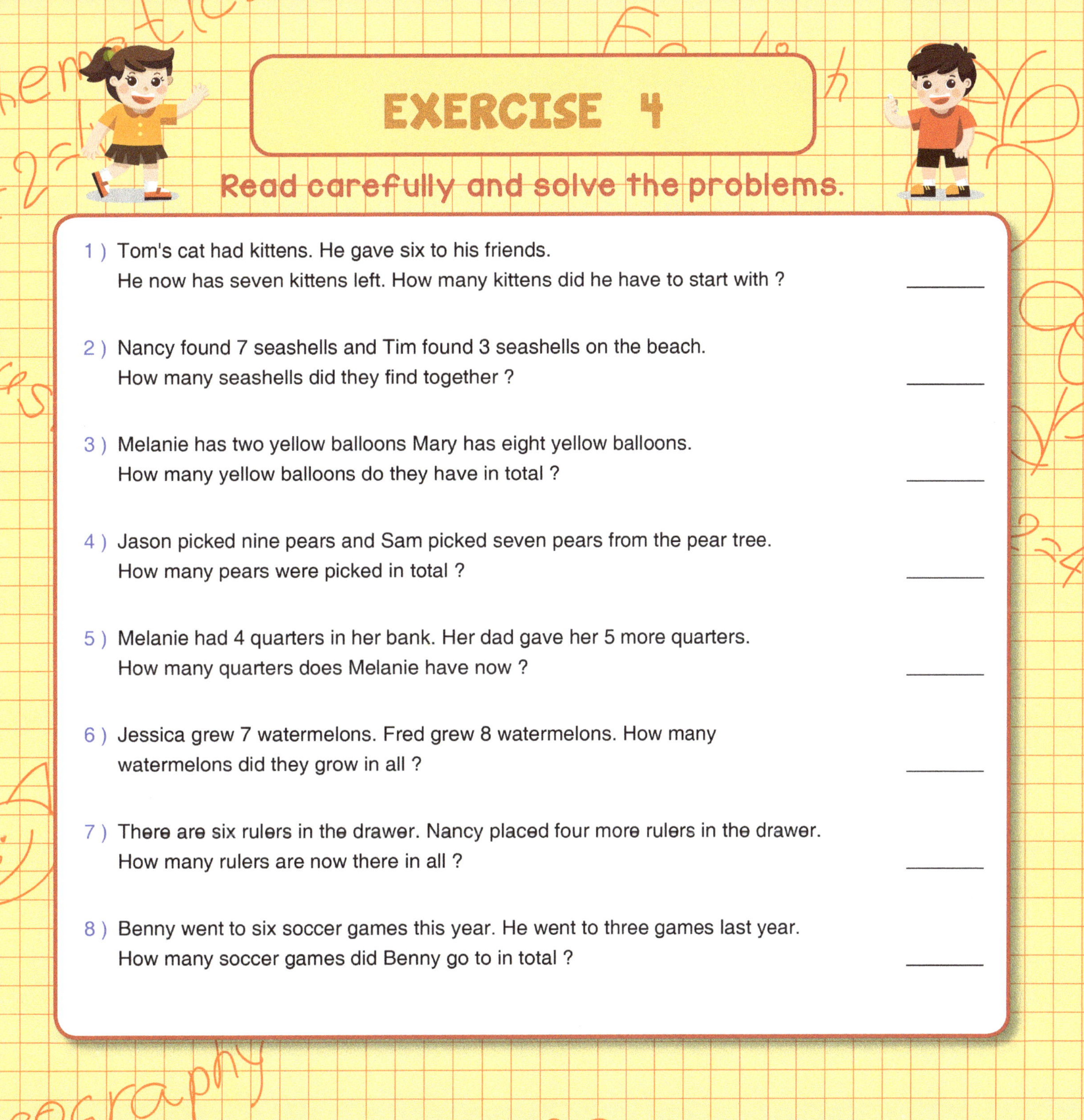

EXERCISE 4

Read carefully and solve the problems.

1) Tom's cat had kittens. He gave six to his friends.
He now has seven kittens left. How many kittens did he have to start with ? ________

2) Nancy found 7 seashells and Tim found 3 seashells on the beach.
How many seashells did they find together ? ________

3) Melanie has two yellow balloons Mary has eight yellow balloons.
How many yellow balloons do they have in total ? ________

4) Jason picked nine pears and Sam picked seven pears from the pear tree.
How many pears were picked in total ? ________

5) Melanie had 4 quarters in her bank. Her dad gave her 5 more quarters.
How many quarters does Melanie have now ? ________

6) Jessica grew 7 watermelons. Fred grew 8 watermelons. How many
watermelons did they grow in all ? ________

7) There are six rulers in the drawer. Nancy placed four more rulers in the drawer.
How many rulers are now there in all ? ________

8) Benny went to six soccer games this year. He went to three games last year.
How many soccer games did Benny go to in total ? ________

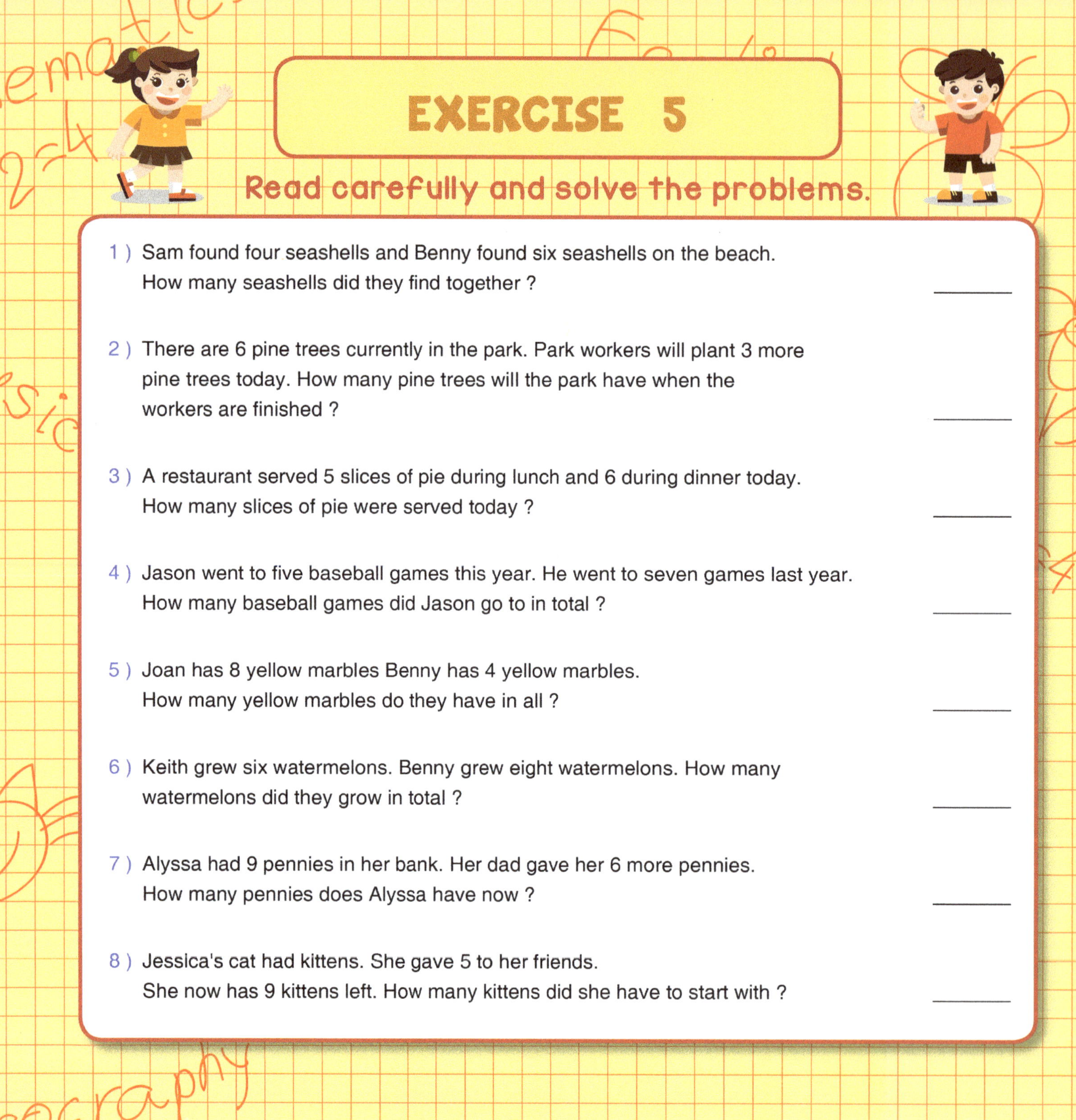

EXERCISE 5

Read carefully and solve the problems.

1) Sam found four seashells and Benny found six seashells on the beach.
How many seashells did they find together ? ________

2) There are 6 pine trees currently in the park. Park workers will plant 3 more
pine trees today. How many pine trees will the park have when the
workers are finished ? ________

3) A restaurant served 5 slices of pie during lunch and 6 during dinner today.
How many slices of pie were served today ? ________

4) Jason went to five baseball games this year. He went to seven games last year.
How many baseball games did Jason go to in total ? ________

5) Joan has 8 yellow marbles Benny has 4 yellow marbles.
How many yellow marbles do they have in all ? ________

6) Keith grew six watermelons. Benny grew eight watermelons. How many
watermelons did they grow in total ? ________

7) Alyssa had 9 pennies in her bank. Her dad gave her 6 more pennies.
How many pennies does Alyssa have now ? ________

8) Jessica's cat had kittens. She gave 5 to her friends.
She now has 9 kittens left. How many kittens did she have to start with ? ________

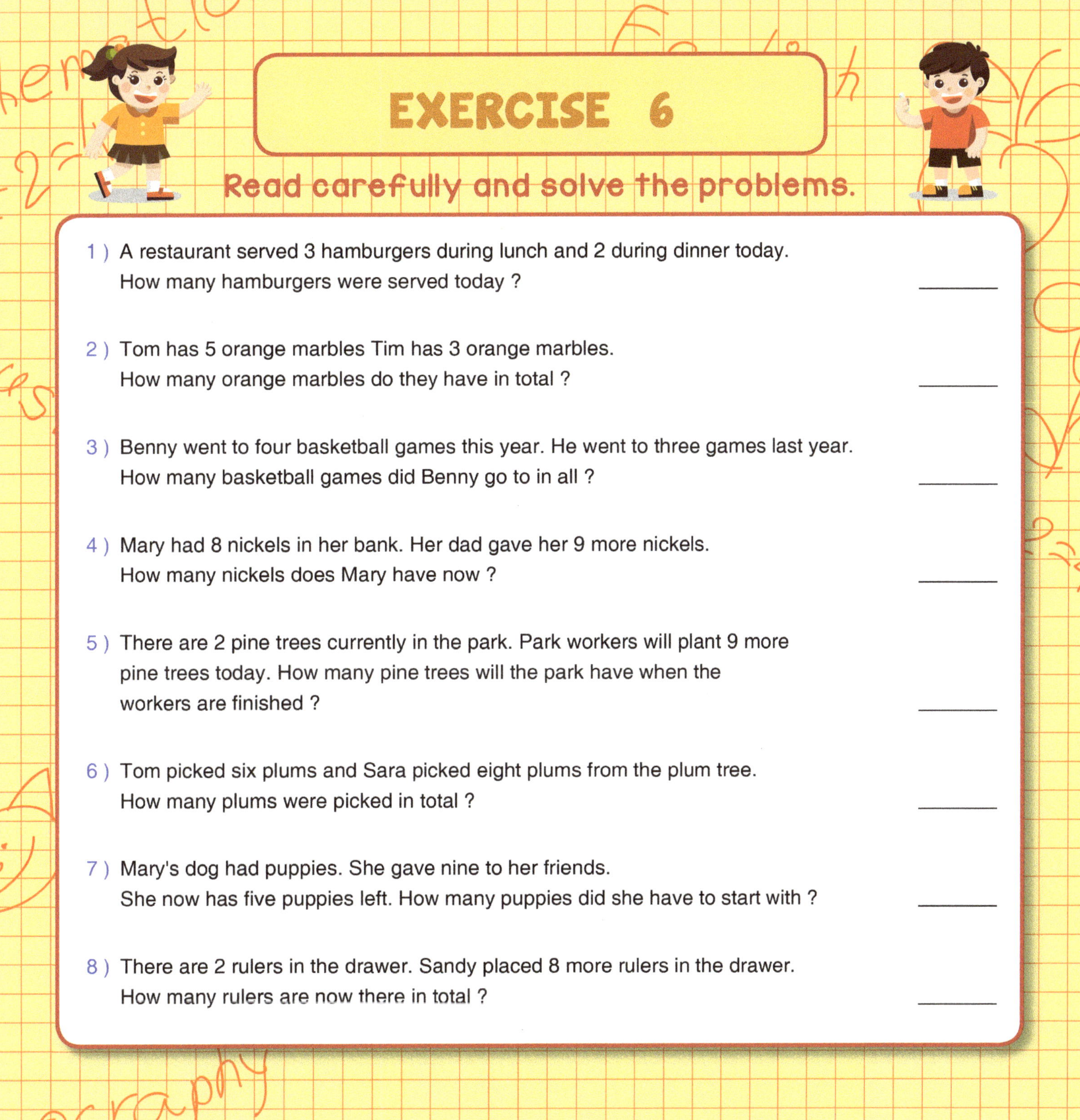

EXERCISE 6

Read carefully and solve the problems.

1) A restaurant served 3 hamburgers during lunch and 2 during dinner today.
How many hamburgers were served today ? ________

2) Tom has 5 orange marbles Tim has 3 orange marbles.
How many orange marbles do they have in total ? ________

3) Benny went to four basketball games this year. He went to three games last year.
How many basketball games did Benny go to in all ? ________

4) Mary had 8 nickels in her bank. Her dad gave her 9 more nickels.
How many nickels does Mary have now ? ________

5) There are 2 pine trees currently in the park. Park workers will plant 9 more
pine trees today. How many pine trees will the park have when the
workers are finished ? ________

6) Tom picked six plums and Sara picked eight plums from the plum tree.
How many plums were picked in total ? ________

7) Mary's dog had puppies. She gave nine to her friends.
She now has five puppies left. How many puppies did she have to start with ? ________

8) There are 2 rulers in the drawer. Sandy placed 8 more rulers in the drawer.
How many rulers are now there in total ? ________

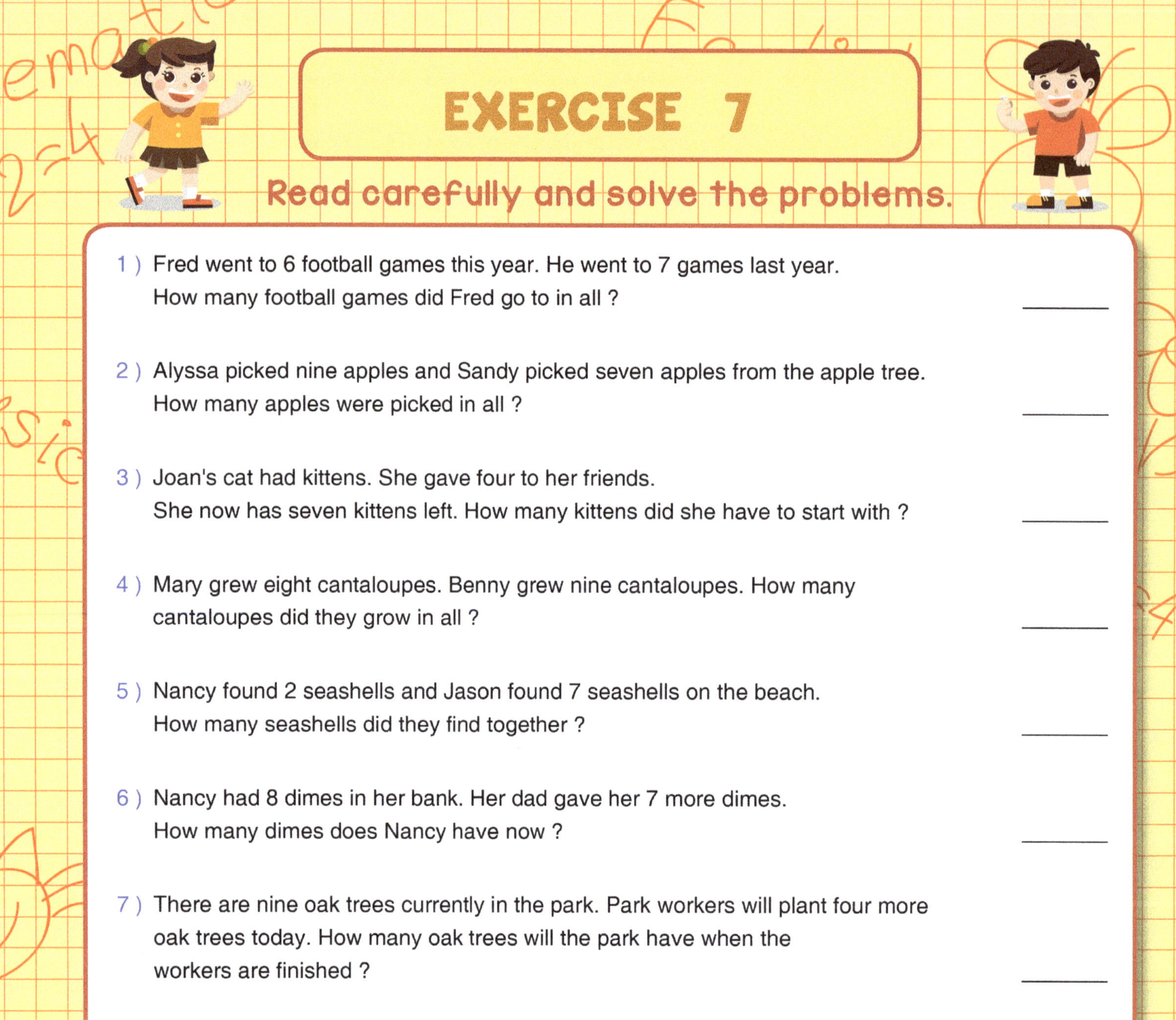

EXERCISE 7

Read carefully and solve the problems.

1) Fred went to 6 football games this year. He went to 7 games last year.
How many football games did Fred go to in all ? ________

2) Alyssa picked nine apples and Sandy picked seven apples from the apple tree.
How many apples were picked in all ? ________

3) Joan's cat had kittens. She gave four to her friends.
She now has seven kittens left. How many kittens did she have to start with ? ________

4) Mary grew eight cantaloupes. Benny grew nine cantaloupes. How many
cantaloupes did they grow in all ? ________

5) Nancy found 2 seashells and Jason found 7 seashells on the beach.
How many seashells did they find together ? ________

6) Nancy had 8 dimes in her bank. Her dad gave her 7 more dimes.
How many dimes does Nancy have now ? ________

7) There are nine oak trees currently in the park. Park workers will plant four more
oak trees today. How many oak trees will the park have when the
workers are finished ? ________

8) Mike has 6 red marbles Sally has 9 red marbles.
How many red marbles do they have in all ? ________

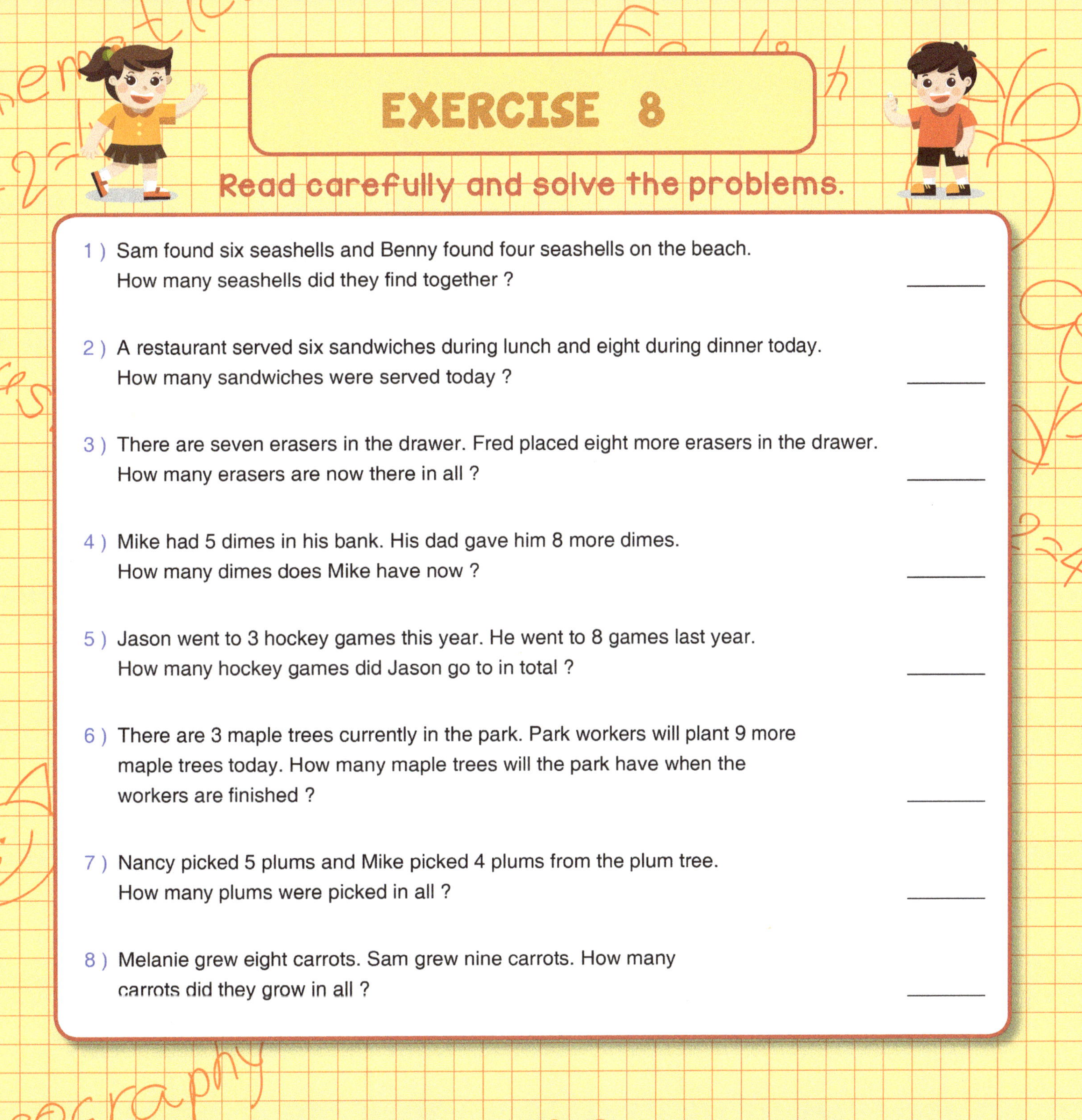

EXERCISE 8

Read carefully and solve the problems.

1) Sam found six seashells and Benny found four seashells on the beach.
How many seashells did they find together ? _________

2) A restaurant served six sandwiches during lunch and eight during dinner today.
How many sandwiches were served today ? _________

3) There are seven erasers in the drawer. Fred placed eight more erasers in the drawer.
How many erasers are now there in all ? _________

4) Mike had 5 dimes in his bank. His dad gave him 8 more dimes.
How many dimes does Mike have now ? _________

5) Jason went to 3 hockey games this year. He went to 8 games last year.
How many hockey games did Jason go to in total ? _________

6) There are 3 maple trees currently in the park. Park workers will plant 9 more
maple trees today. How many maple trees will the park have when the
workers are finished ? _________

7) Nancy picked 5 plums and Mike picked 4 plums from the plum tree.
How many plums were picked in all ? _________

8) Melanie grew eight carrots. Sam grew nine carrots. How many
carrots did they grow in all ? _________

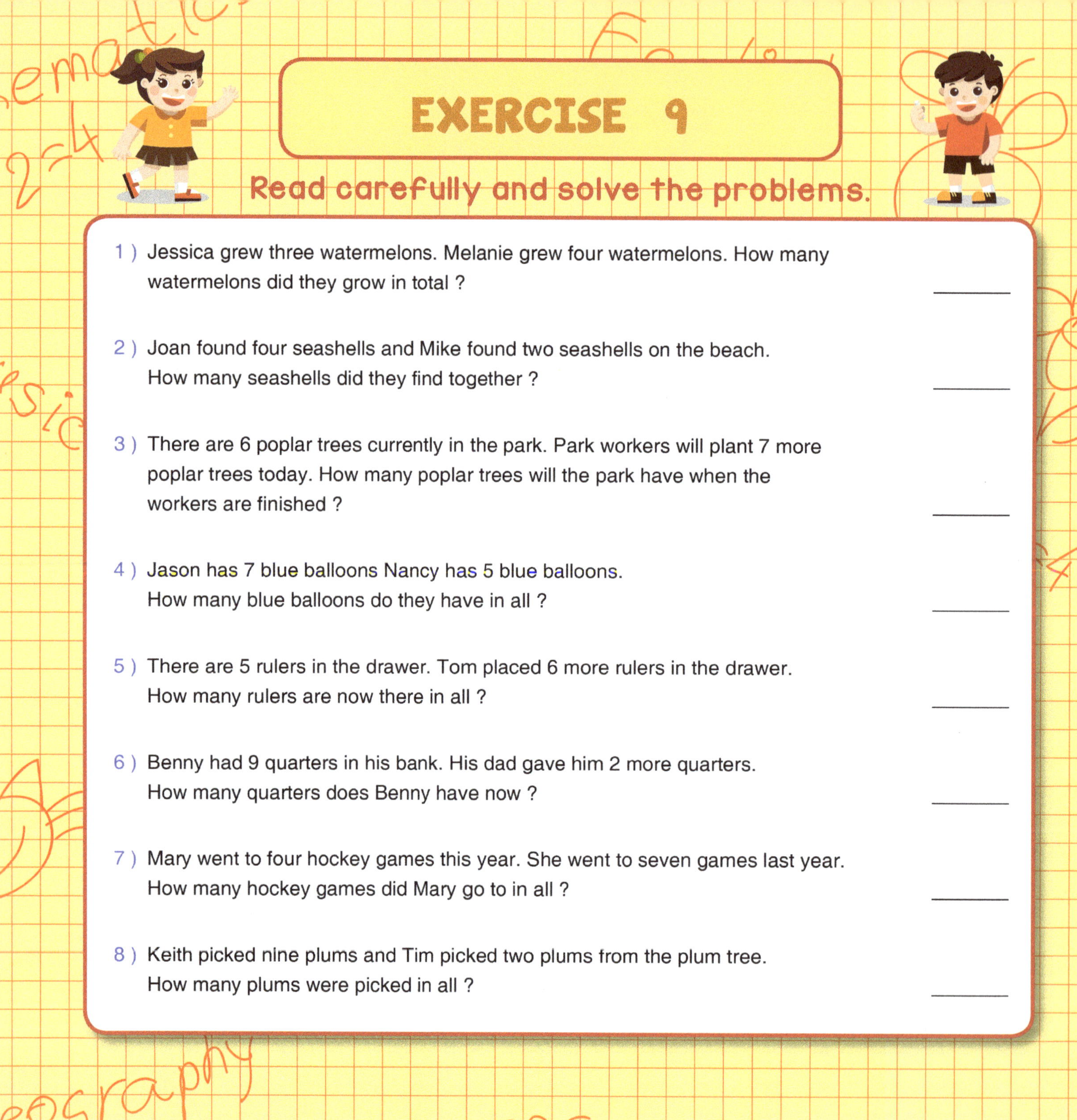

EXERCISE 9

Read carefully and solve the problems.

1) Jessica grew three watermelons. Melanie grew four watermelons. How many watermelons did they grow in total ?

2) Joan found four seashells and Mike found two seashells on the beach. How many seashells did they find together ?

3) There are 6 poplar trees currently in the park. Park workers will plant 7 more poplar trees today. How many poplar trees will the park have when the workers are finished ?

4) Jason has 7 blue balloons Nancy has 5 blue balloons. How many blue balloons do they have in all ?

5) There are 5 rulers in the drawer. Tom placed 6 more rulers in the drawer. How many rulers are now there in all ?

6) Benny had 9 quarters in his bank. His dad gave him 2 more quarters. How many quarters does Benny have now ?

7) Mary went to four hockey games this year. She went to seven games last year. How many hockey games did Mary go to in all ?

8) Keith picked nine plums and Tim picked two plums from the plum tree. How many plums were picked in all ?

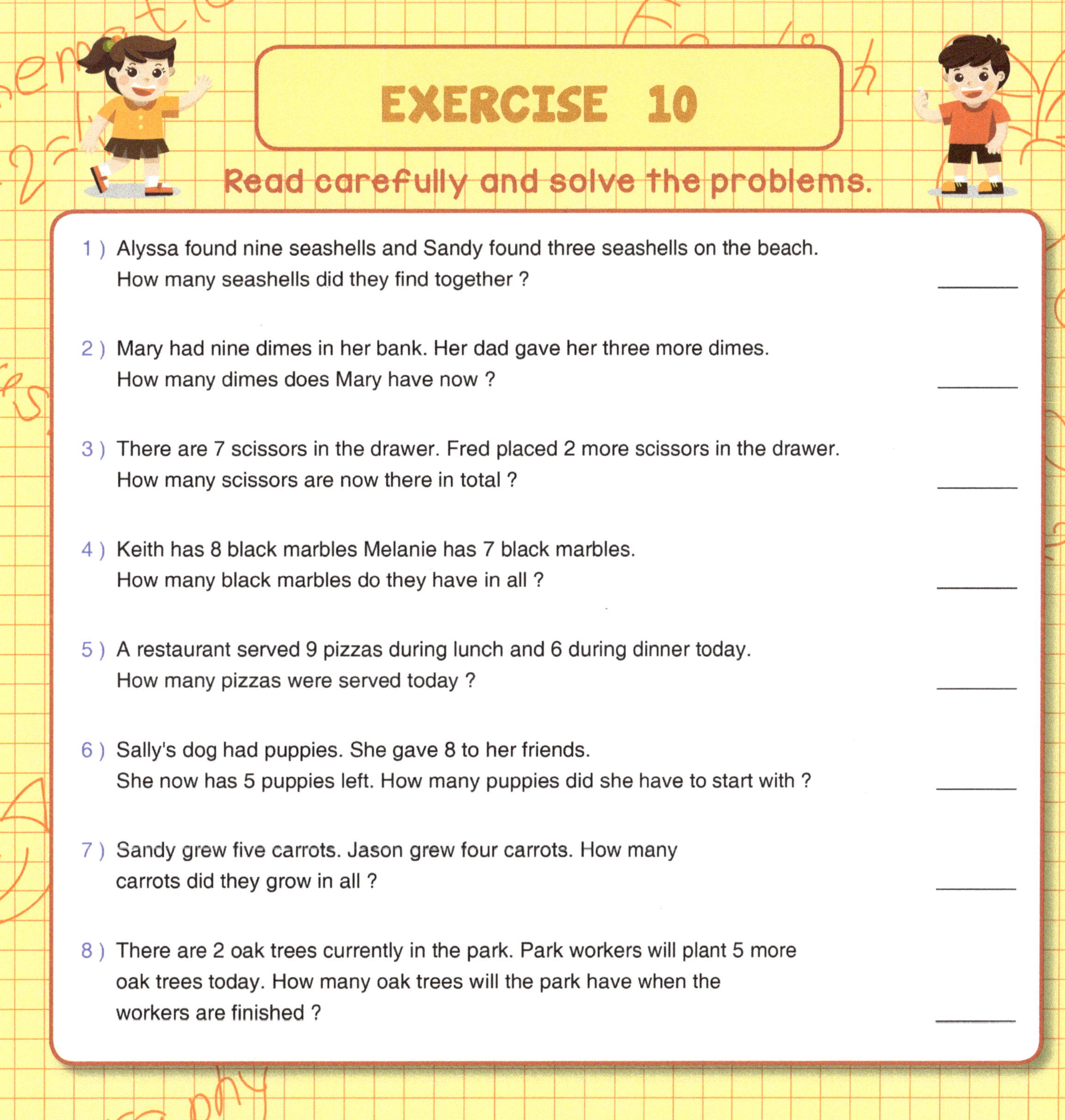

EXERCISE 10

Read carefully and solve the problems.

1) Alyssa found nine seashells and Sandy found three seashells on the beach.
How many seashells did they find together ? ________

2) Mary had nine dimes in her bank. Her dad gave her three more dimes.
How many dimes does Mary have now ? ________

3) There are 7 scissors in the drawer. Fred placed 2 more scissors in the drawer.
How many scissors are now there in total ? ________

4) Keith has 8 black marbles Melanie has 7 black marbles.
How many black marbles do they have in all ? ________

5) A restaurant served 9 pizzas during lunch and 6 during dinner today.
How many pizzas were served today ? ________

6) Sally's dog had puppies. She gave 8 to her friends.
She now has 5 puppies left. How many puppies did she have to start with ? ________

7) Sandy grew five carrots. Jason grew four carrots. How many
carrots did they grow in all ? ________

8) There are 2 oak trees currently in the park. Park workers will plant 5 more
oak trees today. How many oak trees will the park have when the
workers are finished ? ________

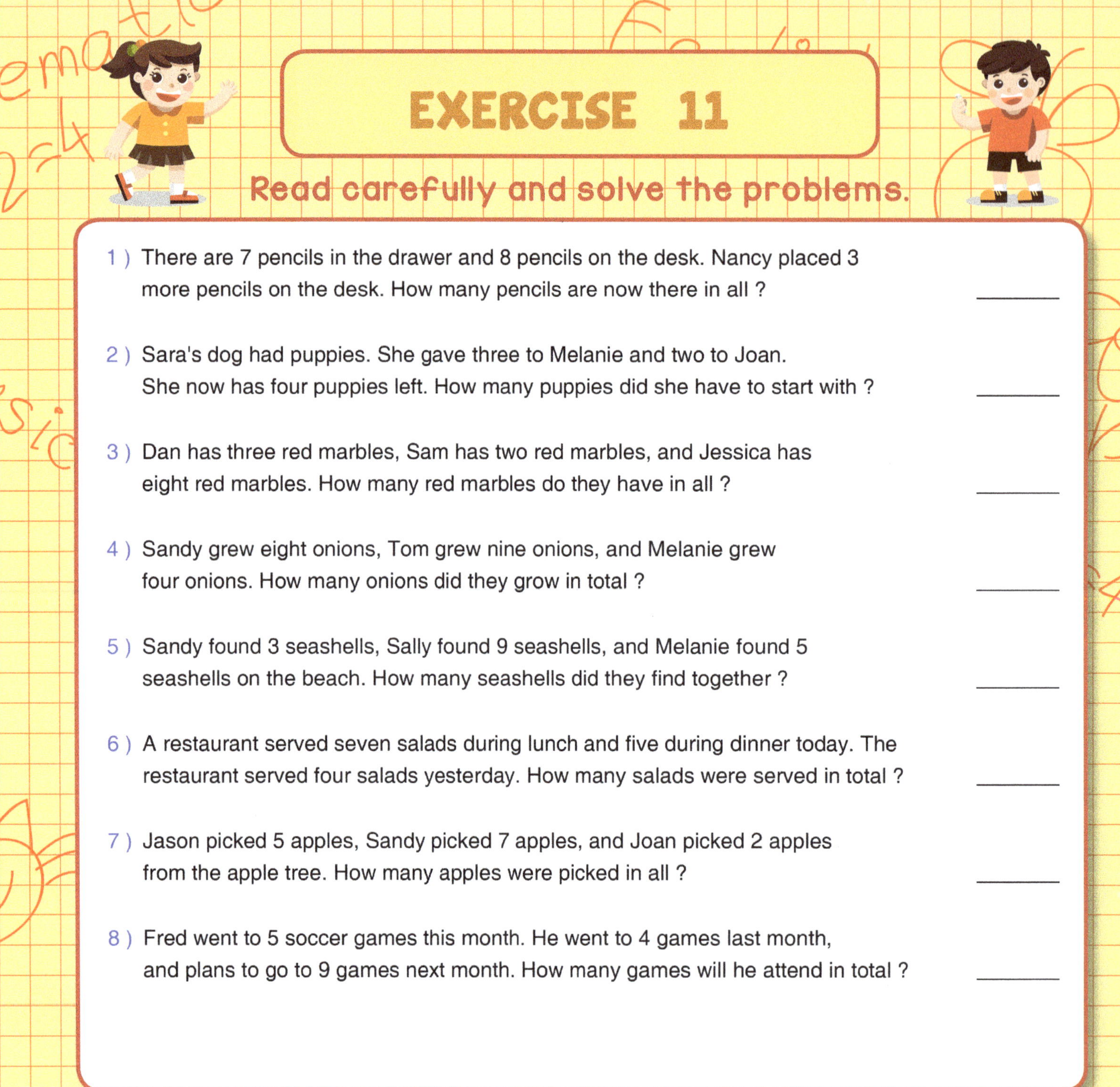

EXERCISE 11

Read carefully and solve the problems.

1) There are 7 pencils in the drawer and 8 pencils on the desk. Nancy placed 3 more pencils on the desk. How many pencils are now there in all ? ________

2) Sara's dog had puppies. She gave three to Melanie and two to Joan. She now has four puppies left. How many puppies did she have to start with ? ________

3) Dan has three red marbles, Sam has two red marbles, and Jessica has eight red marbles. How many red marbles do they have in all ? ________

4) Sandy grew eight onions, Tom grew nine onions, and Melanie grew four onions. How many onions did they grow in total ? ________

5) Sandy found 3 seashells, Sally found 9 seashells, and Melanie found 5 seashells on the beach. How many seashells did they find together ? ________

6) A restaurant served seven salads during lunch and five during dinner today. The restaurant served four salads yesterday. How many salads were served in total ? ________

7) Jason picked 5 apples, Sandy picked 7 apples, and Joan picked 2 apples from the apple tree. How many apples were picked in all ? ________

8) Fred went to 5 soccer games this month. He went to 4 games last month, and plans to go to 9 games next month. How many games will he attend in total ? ________

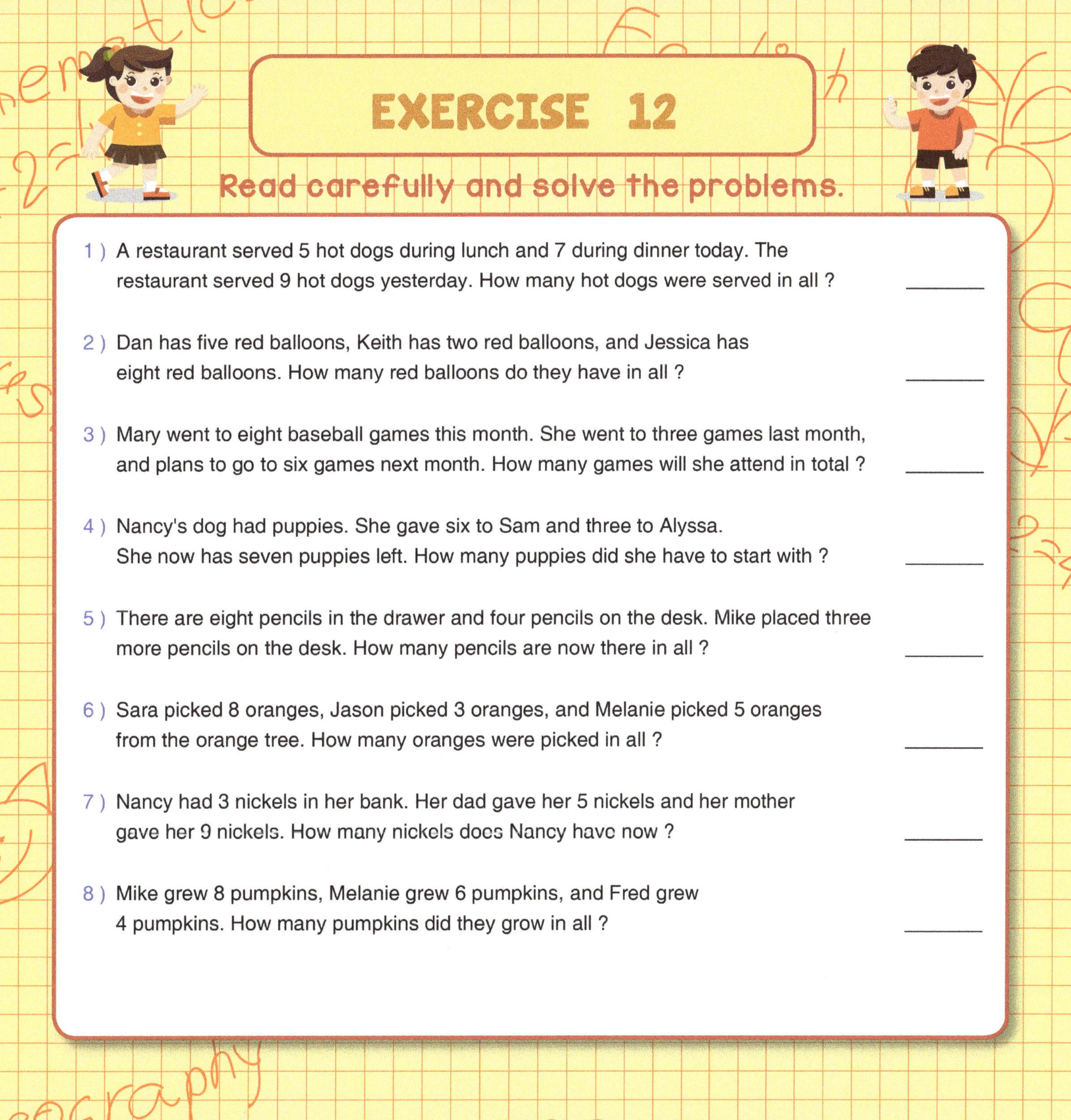

EXERCISE 12

Read carefully and solve the problems.

1) A restaurant served 5 hot dogs during lunch and 7 during dinner today. The restaurant served 9 hot dogs yesterday. How many hot dogs were served in all ? _______

2) Dan has five red balloons, Keith has two red balloons, and Jessica has eight red balloons. How many red balloons do they have in all ? _______

3) Mary went to eight baseball games this month. She went to three games last month, and plans to go to six games next month. How many games will she attend in total ? _______

4) Nancy's dog had puppies. She gave six to Sam and three to Alyssa. She now has seven puppies left. How many puppies did she have to start with ? _______

5) There are eight pencils in the drawer and four pencils on the desk. Mike placed three more pencils on the desk. How many pencils are now there in all ? _______

6) Sara picked 8 oranges, Jason picked 3 oranges, and Melanie picked 5 oranges from the orange tree. How many oranges were picked in all ? _______

7) Nancy had 3 nickels in her bank. Her dad gave her 5 nickels and her mother gave her 9 nickels. How many nickels does Nancy have now ? _______

8) Mike grew 8 pumpkins, Melanie grew 6 pumpkins, and Fred grew 4 pumpkins. How many pumpkins did they grow in all ? _______

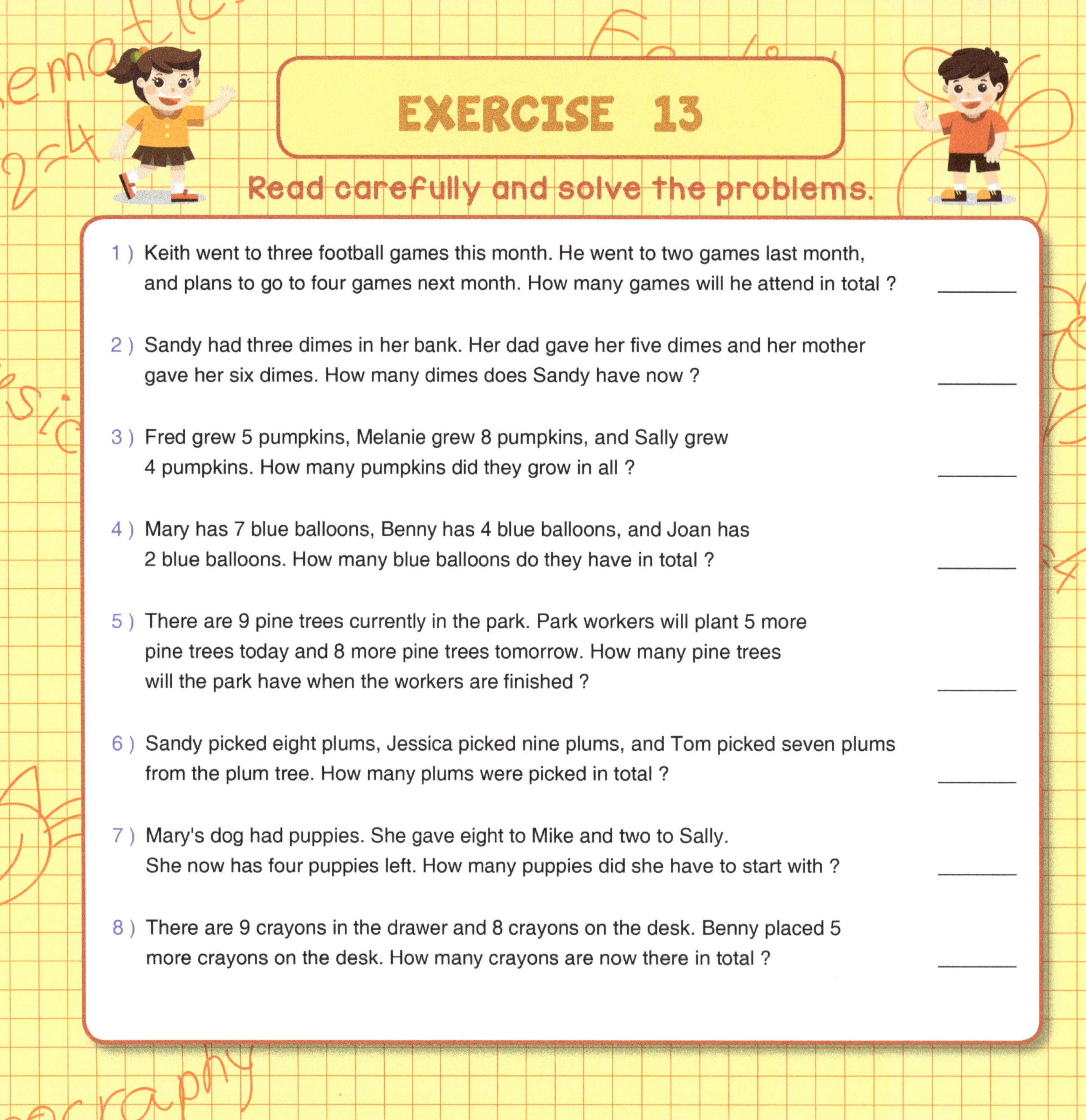

1) Keith went to three football games this month. He went to two games last month, and plans to go to four games next month. How many games will he attend in total ?   ________

2) Sandy had three dimes in her bank. Her dad gave her five dimes and her mother gave her six dimes. How many dimes does Sandy have now ?   ________

3) Fred grew 5 pumpkins, Melanie grew 8 pumpkins, and Sally grew 4 pumpkins. How many pumpkins did they grow in all ?   ________

4) Mary has 7 blue balloons, Benny has 4 blue balloons, and Joan has 2 blue balloons. How many blue balloons do they have in total ?   ________

5) There are 9 pine trees currently in the park. Park workers will plant 5 more pine trees today and 8 more pine trees tomorrow. How many pine trees will the park have when the workers are finished ?   ________

6) Sandy picked eight plums, Jessica picked nine plums, and Tom picked seven plums from the plum tree. How many plums were picked in total ?   ________

7) Mary's dog had puppies. She gave eight to Mike and two to Sally. She now has four puppies left. How many puppies did she have to start with ?   ________

8) There are 9 crayons in the drawer and 8 crayons on the desk. Benny placed 5 more crayons on the desk. How many crayons are now there in total ?   ________

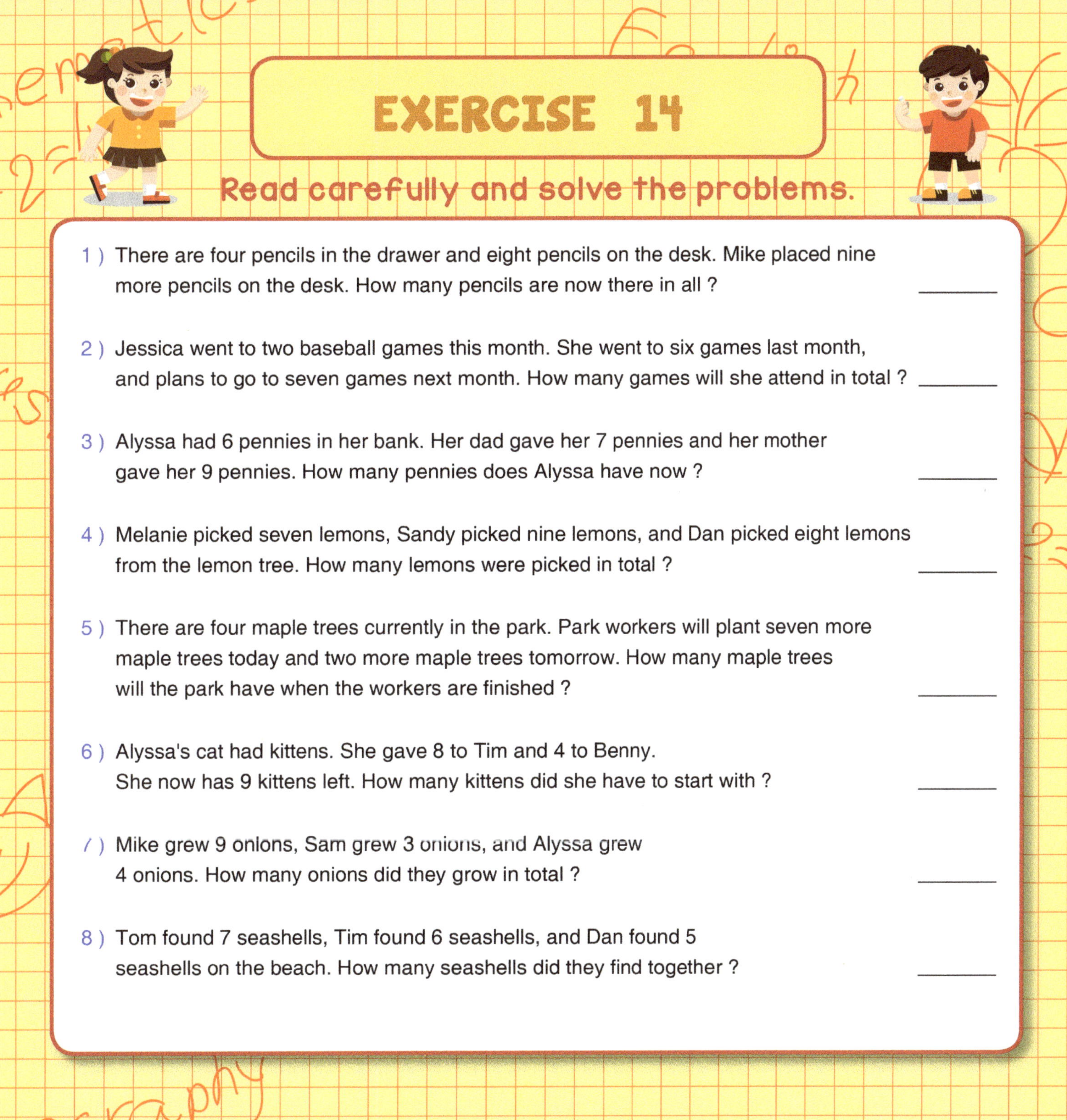

EXERCISE 14

Read carefully and solve the problems.

1) There are four pencils in the drawer and eight pencils on the desk. Mike placed nine more pencils on the desk. How many pencils are now there in all ? _______

2) Jessica went to two baseball games this month. She went to six games last month, and plans to go to seven games next month. How many games will she attend in total ? _______

3) Alyssa had 6 pennies in her bank. Her dad gave her 7 pennies and her mother gave her 9 pennies. How many pennies does Alyssa have now ? _______

4) Melanie picked seven lemons, Sandy picked nine lemons, and Dan picked eight lemons from the lemon tree. How many lemons were picked in total ? _______

5) There are four maple trees currently in the park. Park workers will plant seven more maple trees today and two more maple trees tomorrow. How many maple trees will the park have when the workers are finished ? _______

6) Alyssa's cat had kittens. She gave 8 to Tim and 4 to Benny. She now has 9 kittens left. How many kittens did she have to start with ? _______

7) Mike grew 9 onions, Sam grew 3 onions, and Alyssa grew 4 onions. How many onions did they grow in total ? _______

8) Tom found 7 seashells, Tim found 6 seashells, and Dan found 5 seashells on the beach. How many seashells did they find together ? _______

EXERCISE 15

Read carefully and solve the problems.

1) There are six dogwood trees currently in the park. Park workers will plant four more dogwood trees today and five more dogwood trees tomorrow. How many dogwood trees will the park have when the workers are finished ? ________

2) Keith had 2 quarters in his bank. His dad gave him 9 quarters and his mother gave him 7 quarters. How many quarters does Keith have now ? ________

3) Sally's dog had puppies. She gave seven to Mary and two to Mike. She now has eight puppies left. How many puppies did she have to start with ? ________

4) There are 6 scissors in the drawer and 2 scissors on the desk. Dan placed 9 more scissors on the desk. How many scissors are now there in all ? ________

5) Melanie has three orange marbles, Tom has seven orange marbles, and Alyssa has nine orange marbles. How many orange marbles do they have in total ? ________

6) Melanie grew six carrots, Nancy grew four carrots, and Joan grew seven carrots. How many carrots did they grow in all ? ________

7) A restaurant served 3 pies during lunch and 2 during dinner today. The restaurant served 7 pies yesterday. How many pies were served in total ? ________

8) Jessica found 5 seashells, Mary found 9 seashells, and Tom found 6 seashells on the beach. How many seashells did they find together ? ________

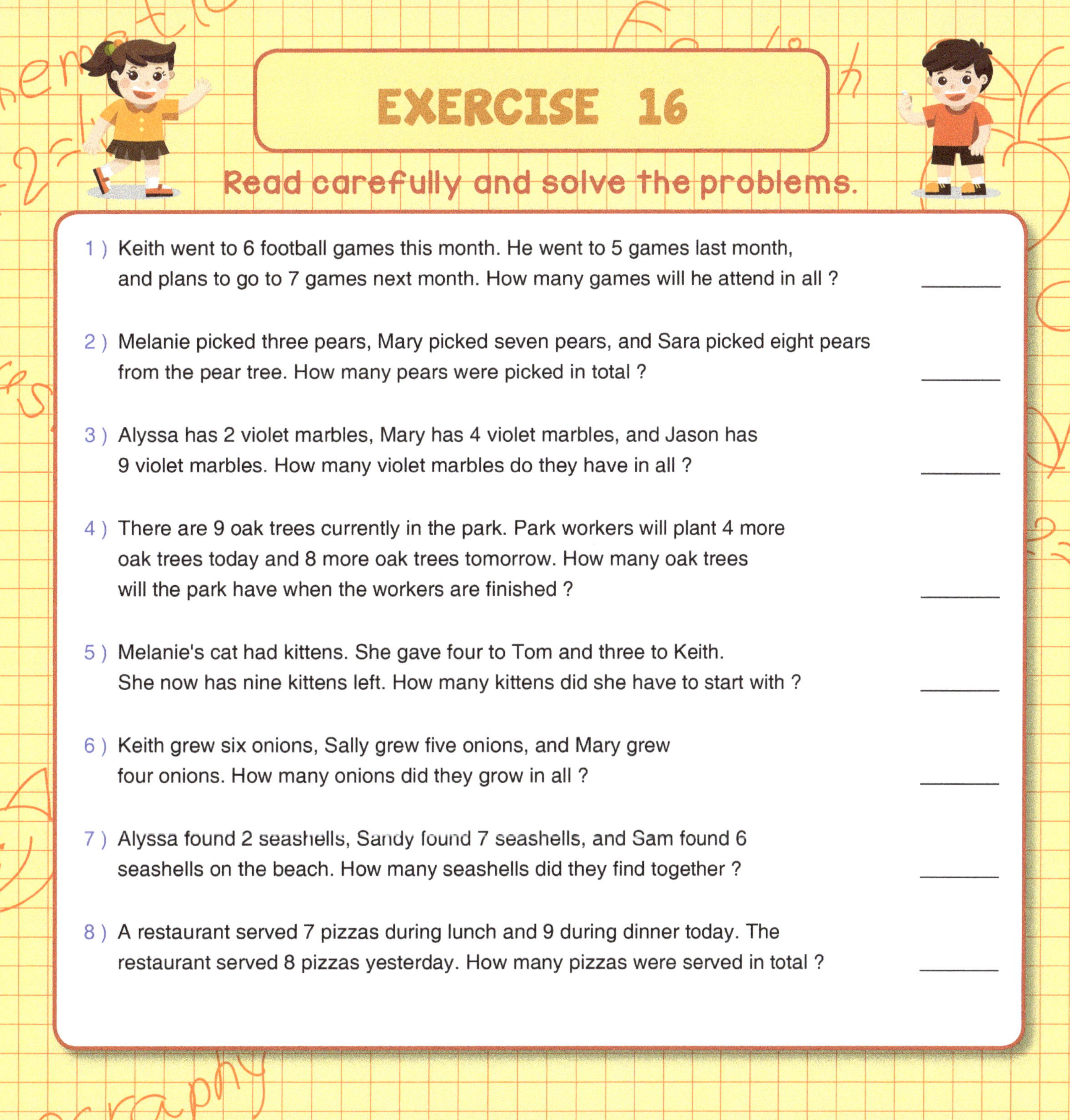

EXERCISE 16

Read carefully and solve the problems.

1) Keith went to 6 football games this month. He went to 5 games last month, and plans to go to 7 games next month. How many games will he attend in all ? ________

2) Melanie picked three pears, Mary picked seven pears, and Sara picked eight pears from the pear tree. How many pears were picked in total ? ________

3) Alyssa has 2 violet marbles, Mary has 4 violet marbles, and Jason has 9 violet marbles. How many violet marbles do they have in all ? ________

4) There are 9 oak trees currently in the park. Park workers will plant 4 more oak trees today and 8 more oak trees tomorrow. How many oak trees will the park have when the workers are finished ? ________

5) Melanie's cat had kittens. She gave four to Tom and three to Keith. She now has nine kittens left. How many kittens did she have to start with ? ________

6) Keith grew six onions, Sally grew five onions, and Mary grew four onions. How many onions did they grow in all ? ________

7) Alyssa found 2 seashells, Sandy found 7 seashells, and Sam found 6 seashells on the beach. How many seashells did they find together ? ________

8) A restaurant served 7 pizzas during lunch and 9 during dinner today. The restaurant served 8 pizzas yesterday. How many pizzas were served in total ? ________

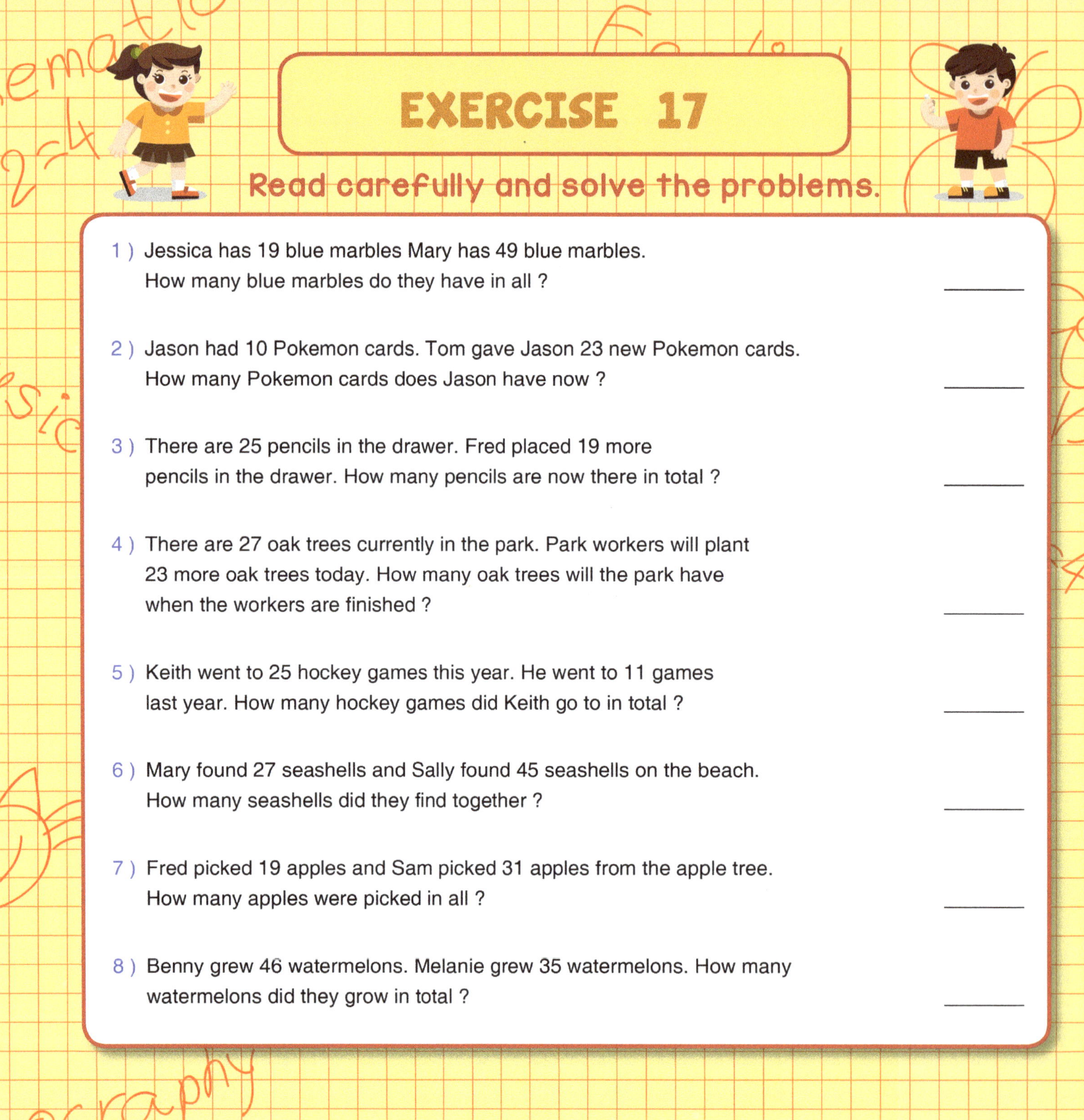

EXERCISE 17

Read carefully and solve the problems.

1) Jessica has 19 blue marbles Mary has 49 blue marbles.
How many blue marbles do they have in all ?   _________

2) Jason had 10 Pokemon cards. Tom gave Jason 23 new Pokemon cards.
How many Pokemon cards does Jason have now ?   _________

3) There are 25 pencils in the drawer. Fred placed 19 more
pencils in the drawer. How many pencils are now there in total ?   _________

4) There are 27 oak trees currently in the park. Park workers will plant
23 more oak trees today. How many oak trees will the park have
when the workers are finished ?   _________

5) Keith went to 25 hockey games this year. He went to 11 games
last year. How many hockey games did Keith go to in total ?   _________

6) Mary found 27 seashells and Sally found 45 seashells on the beach.
How many seashells did they find together ?   _________

7) Fred picked 19 apples and Sam picked 31 apples from the apple tree.
How many apples were picked in all ?   _________

8) Benny grew 46 watermelons. Melanie grew 35 watermelons. How many
watermelons did they grow in total ?   _________

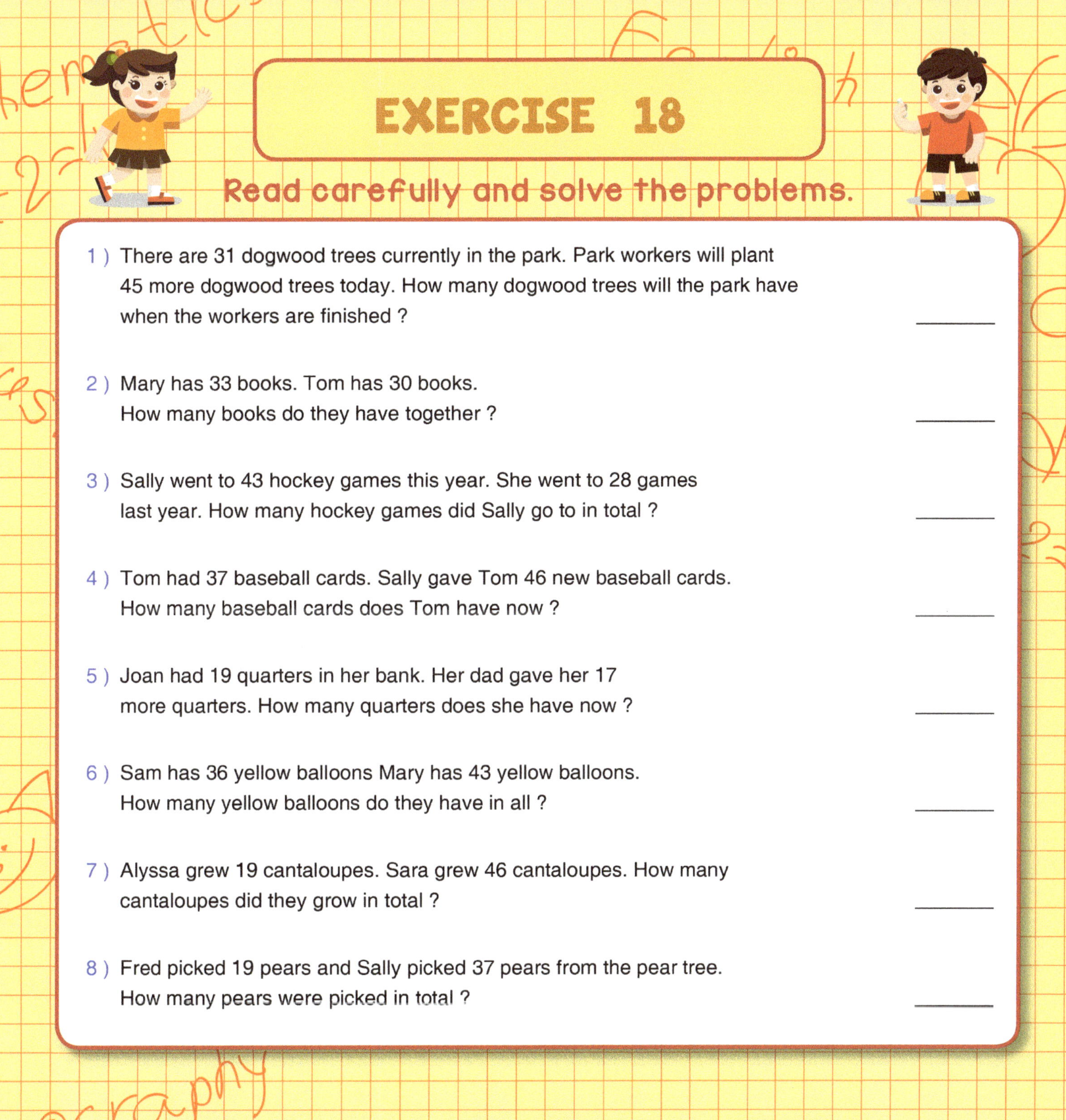

EXERCISE 18

Read carefully and solve the problems.

1) There are 31 dogwood trees currently in the park. Park workers will plant 45 more dogwood trees today. How many dogwood trees will the park have when the workers are finished ?   ________

2) Mary has 33 books. Tom has 30 books.
How many books do they have together ?   ________

3) Sally went to 43 hockey games this year. She went to 28 games last year. How many hockey games did Sally go to in total ?   ________

4) Tom had 37 baseball cards. Sally gave Tom 46 new baseball cards. How many baseball cards does Tom have now ?   ________

5) Joan had 19 quarters in her bank. Her dad gave her 17 more quarters. How many quarters does she have now ?   ________

6) Sam has 36 yellow balloons Mary has 43 yellow balloons. How many yellow balloons do they have in all ?   ________

7) Alyssa grew 19 cantaloupes. Sara grew 46 cantaloupes. How many cantaloupes did they grow in total ?   ________

8) Fred picked 19 pears and Sally picked 37 pears from the pear tree. How many pears were picked in total ?   ________

EXERCISE 19

Read carefully and solve the problems.

1) Alyssa picked 33 apples and Melanie picked 36 apples from the apple tree.
How many apples were picked in total ? _________

2) Benny grew 26 pumpkins. Melanie grew 20 pumpkins. How many
pumpkins did they grow in all ? _________

3) Sara had 12 dimes in her bank. Her dad gave her 34
more dimes. How many dimes does she have now ? _________

4) Nancy had 10 Pokemon cards. Sally gave Nancy 23 new Pokemon cards.
How many Pokemon cards does Nancy have now ? _________

5) Keith has 48 books. Tom has 28 books.
How many books do they have together ? _________

6) There are 26 poplar trees currently in the park. Park workers will plant
14 more poplar trees today. How many poplar trees will the park have
when the workers are finished ? _________

7) Dan went to 49 football games this year. He went to 45 games
last year. How many football games did Dan go to in total ? _________

8) Jessica has 20 red marbles Jason has 48 red marbles.
How many red marbles do they have in all ? _________

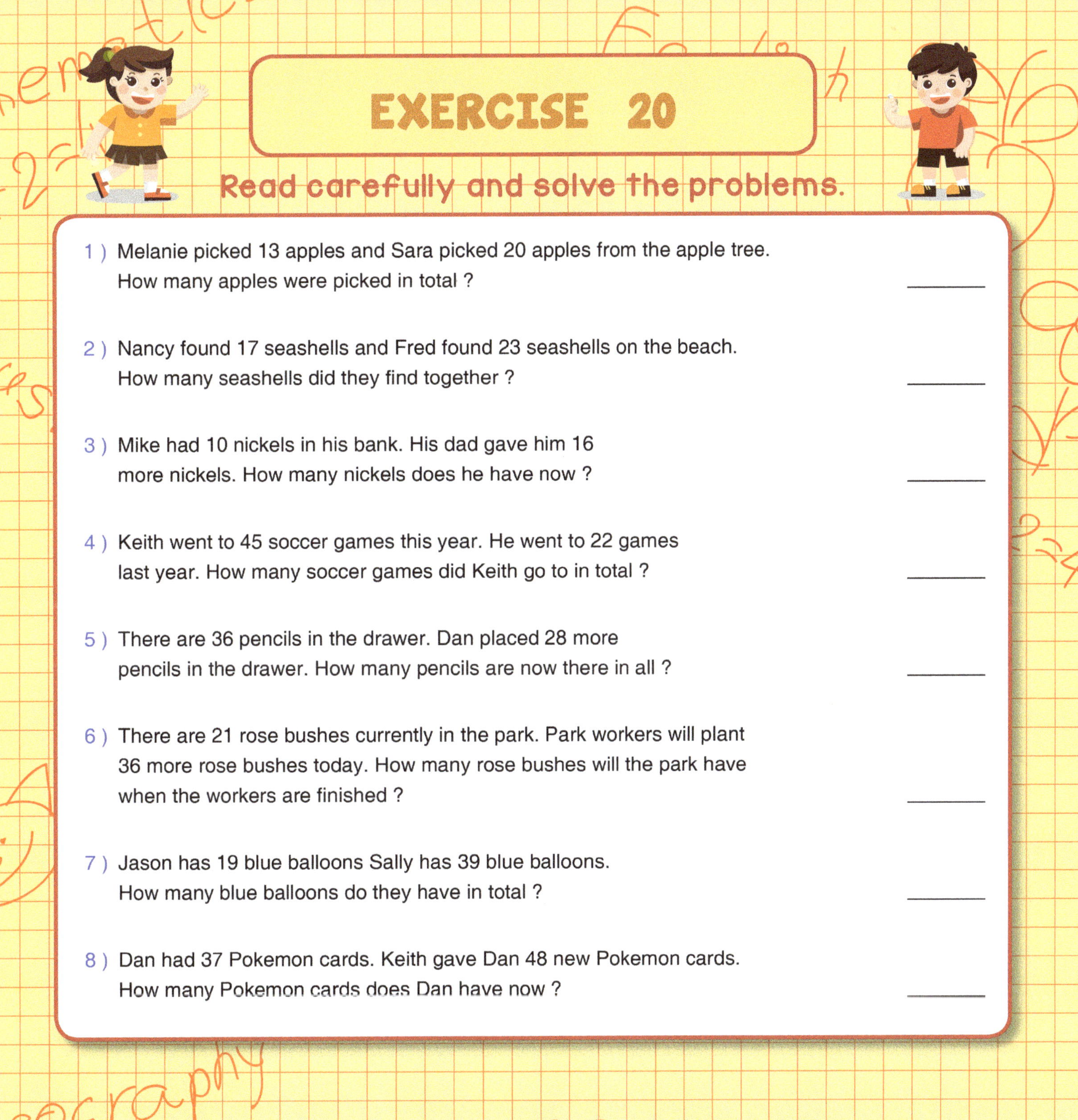

EXERCISE 20

Read carefully and solve the problems.

1) Melanie picked 13 apples and Sara picked 20 apples from the apple tree. How many apples were picked in total ? _______

2) Nancy found 17 seashells and Fred found 23 seashells on the beach. How many seashells did they find together ? _______

3) Mike had 10 nickels in his bank. His dad gave him 16 more nickels. How many nickels does he have now ? _______

4) Keith went to 45 soccer games this year. He went to 22 games last year. How many soccer games did Keith go to in total ? _______

5) There are 36 pencils in the drawer. Dan placed 28 more pencils in the drawer. How many pencils are now there in all ? _______

6) There are 21 rose bushes currently in the park. Park workers will plant 36 more rose bushes today. How many rose bushes will the park have when the workers are finished ? _______

7) Jason has 19 blue balloons Sally has 39 blue balloons. How many blue balloons do they have in total ? _______

8) Dan had 37 Pokemon cards. Keith gave Dan 48 new Pokemon cards. How many Pokemon cards does Dan have now ? _______

HI KIDS!

Help us solve these easy subtraction word problems.

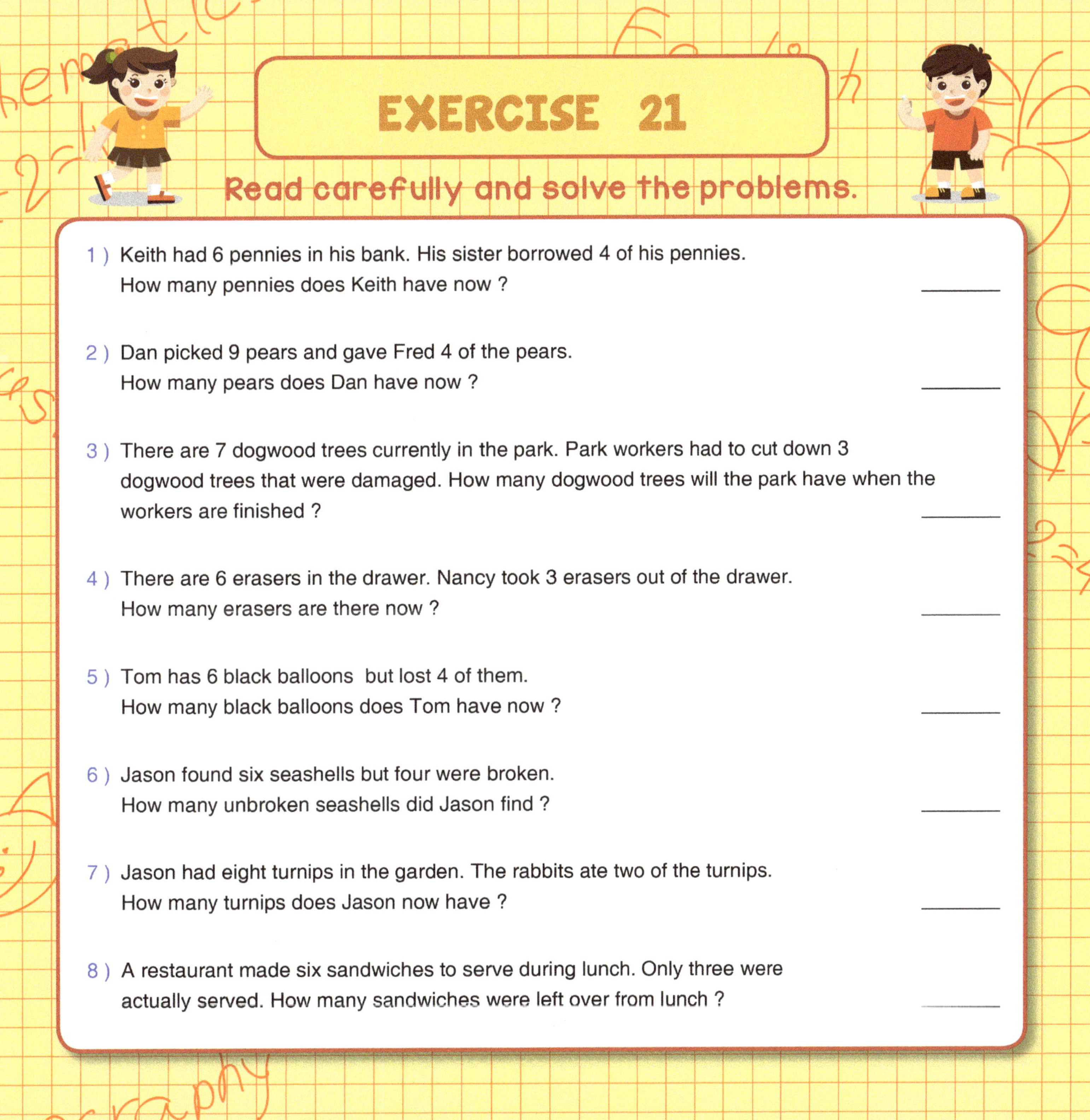

EXERCISE 21

Read carefully and solve the problems.

1) Keith had 6 pennies in his bank. His sister borrowed 4 of his pennies.
How many pennies does Keith have now ? ________

2) Dan picked 9 pears and gave Fred 4 of the pears.
How many pears does Dan have now ? ________

3) There are 7 dogwood trees currently in the park. Park workers had to cut down 3
dogwood trees that were damaged. How many dogwood trees will the park have when the
workers are finished ? ________

4) There are 6 erasers in the drawer. Nancy took 3 erasers out of the drawer.
How many erasers are there now ? ________

5) Tom has 6 black balloons but lost 4 of them.
How many black balloons does Tom have now ? ________

6) Jason found six seashells but four were broken.
How many unbroken seashells did Jason find ? ________

7) Jason had eight turnips in the garden. The rabbits ate two of the turnips.
How many turnips does Jason now have ? ________

8) A restaurant made six sandwiches to serve during lunch. Only three were
actually served. How many sandwiches were left over from lunch ? ________

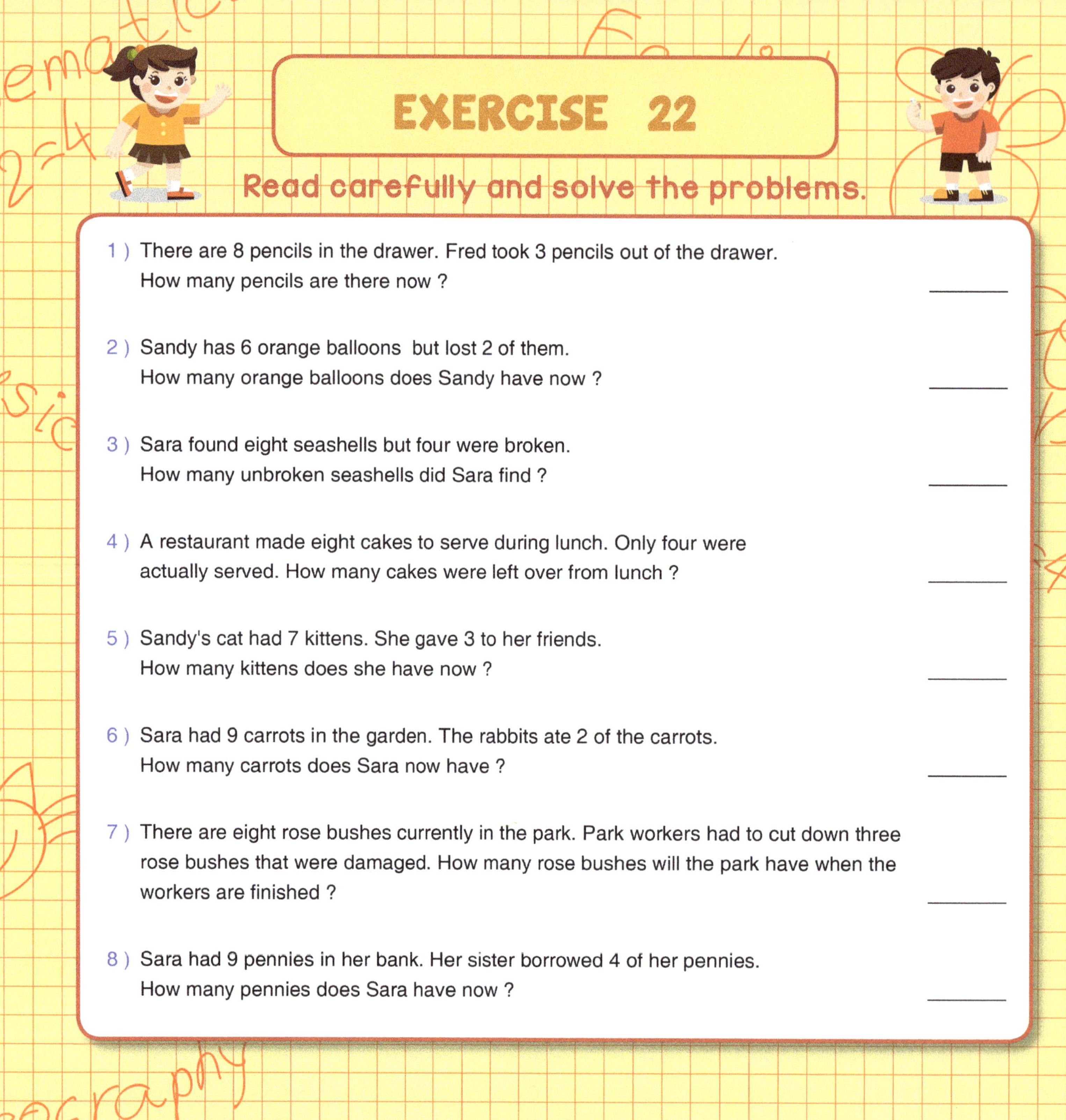

EXERCISE 22

Read carefully and solve the problems.

1) There are 8 pencils in the drawer. Fred took 3 pencils out of the drawer.
How many pencils are there now ? ________

2) Sandy has 6 orange balloons but lost 2 of them.
How many orange balloons does Sandy have now ? ________

3) Sara found eight seashells but four were broken.
How many unbroken seashells did Sara find ? ________

4) A restaurant made eight cakes to serve during lunch. Only four were
actually served. How many cakes were left over from lunch ? ________

5) Sandy's cat had 7 kittens. She gave 3 to her friends.
How many kittens does she have now ? ________

6) Sara had 9 carrots in the garden. The rabbits ate 2 of the carrots.
How many carrots does Sara now have ? ________

7) There are eight rose bushes currently in the park. Park workers had to cut down three
rose bushes that were damaged. How many rose bushes will the park have when the
workers are finished ? ________

8) Sara had 9 pennies in her bank. Her sister borrowed 4 of her pennies.
How many pennies does Sara have now ? ________

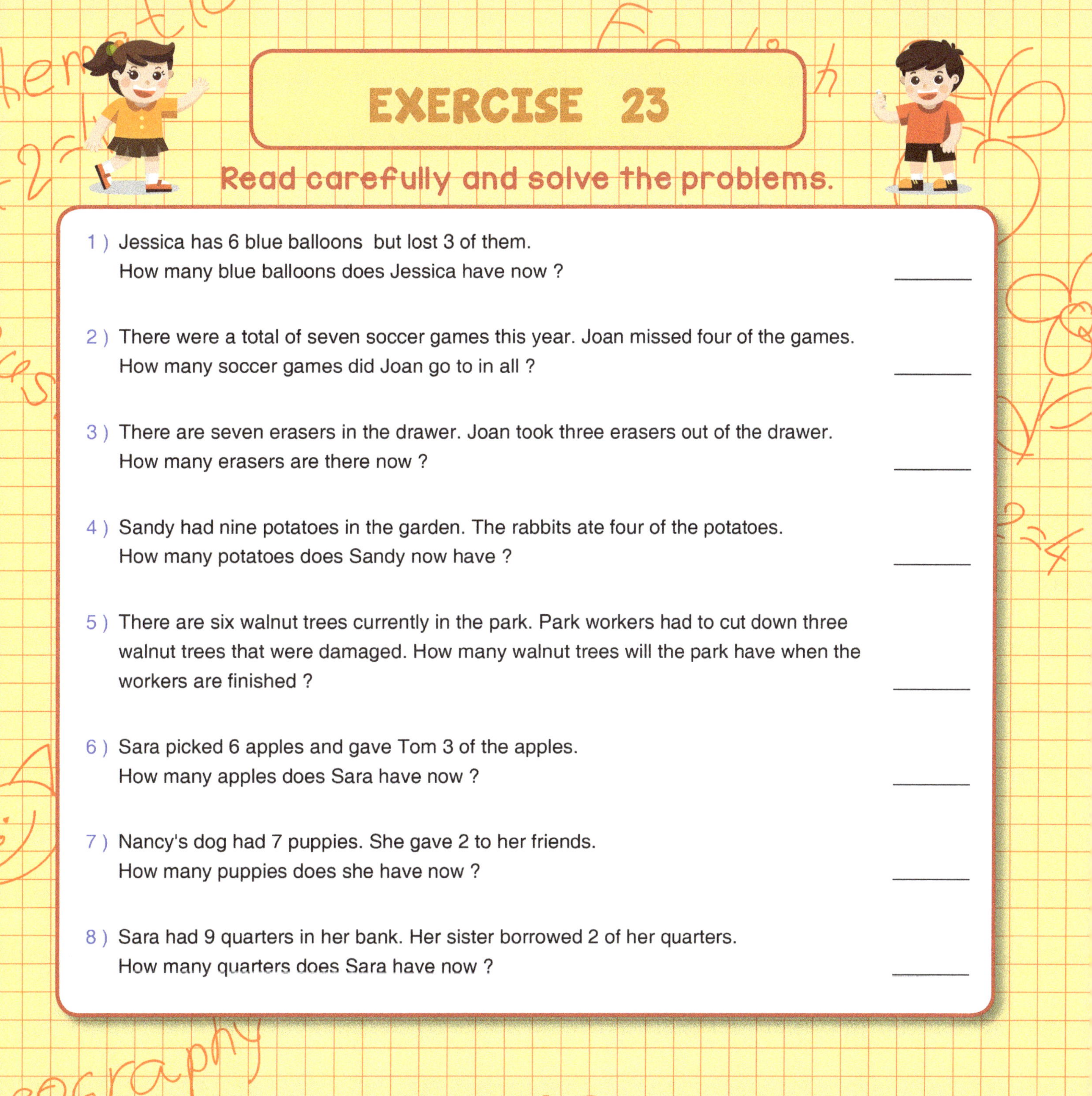

EXERCISE 23

Read carefully and solve the problems.

1) Jessica has 6 blue balloons but lost 3 of them.
How many blue balloons does Jessica have now ? ________

2) There were a total of seven soccer games this year. Joan missed four of the games.
How many soccer games did Joan go to in all ? ________

3) There are seven erasers in the drawer. Joan took three erasers out of the drawer.
How many erasers are there now ? ________

4) Sandy had nine potatoes in the garden. The rabbits ate four of the potatoes.
How many potatoes does Sandy now have ? ________

5) There are six walnut trees currently in the park. Park workers had to cut down three
walnut trees that were damaged. How many walnut trees will the park have when the
workers are finished ? ________

6) Sara picked 6 apples and gave Tom 3 of the apples.
How many apples does Sara have now ? ________

7) Nancy's dog had 7 puppies. She gave 2 to her friends.
How many puppies does she have now ? ________

8) Sara had 9 quarters in her bank. Her sister borrowed 2 of her quarters.
How many quarters does Sara have now ? ________

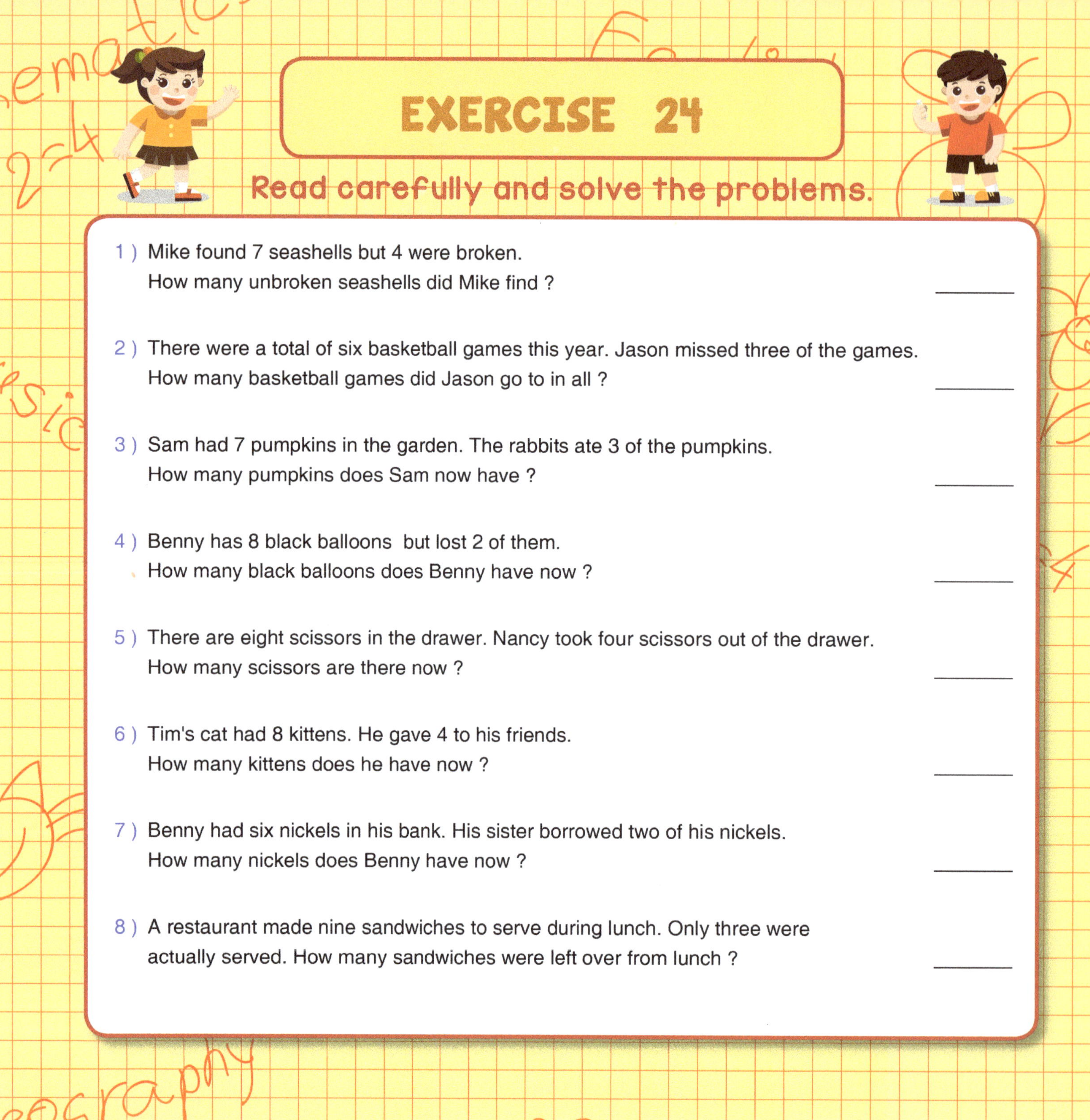

EXERCISE 24

Read carefully and solve the problems.

1) Mike found 7 seashells but 4 were broken.
How many unbroken seashells did Mike find ? ________

2) There were a total of six basketball games this year. Jason missed three of the games.
How many basketball games did Jason go to in all ? ________

3) Sam had 7 pumpkins in the garden. The rabbits ate 3 of the pumpkins.
How many pumpkins does Sam now have ? ________

4) Benny has 8 black balloons but lost 2 of them.
How many black balloons does Benny have now ? ________

5) There are eight scissors in the drawer. Nancy took four scissors out of the drawer.
How many scissors are there now ? ________

6) Tim's cat had 8 kittens. He gave 4 to his friends.
How many kittens does he have now ? ________

7) Benny had six nickels in his bank. His sister borrowed two of his nickels.
How many nickels does Benny have now ? ________

8) A restaurant made nine sandwiches to serve during lunch. Only three were
actually served. How many sandwiches were left over from lunch ? ________

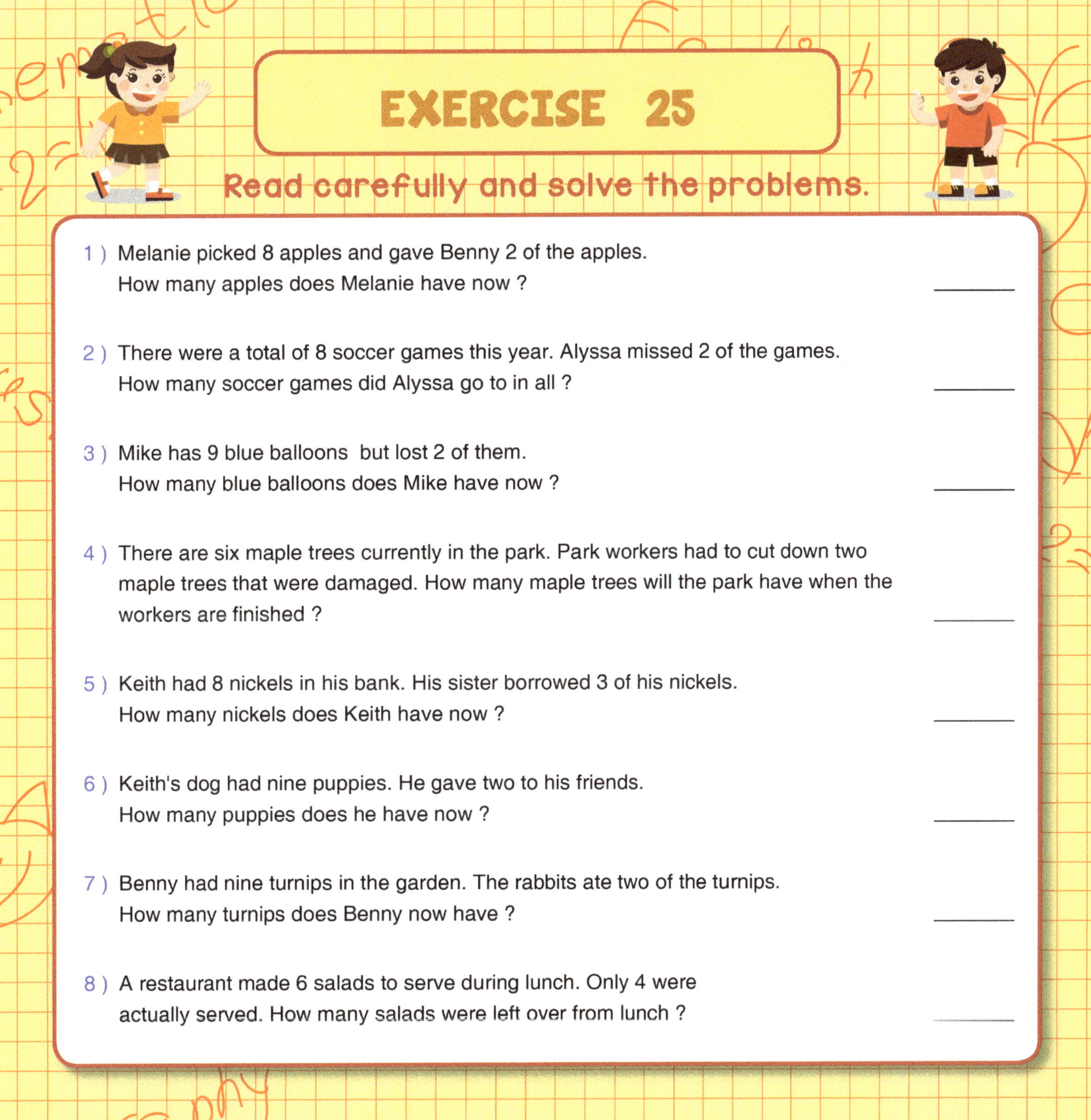

EXERCISE 25

Read carefully and solve the problems.

1) Melanie picked 8 apples and gave Benny 2 of the apples.
How many apples does Melanie have now ?   ________

2) There were a total of 8 soccer games this year. Alyssa missed 2 of the games.
How many soccer games did Alyssa go to in all ?   ________

3) Mike has 9 blue balloons but lost 2 of them.
How many blue balloons does Mike have now ?   ________

4) There are six maple trees currently in the park. Park workers had to cut down two
maple trees that were damaged. How many maple trees will the park have when the
workers are finished ?   ________

5) Keith had 8 nickels in his bank. His sister borrowed 3 of his nickels.
How many nickels does Keith have now ?   ________

6) Keith's dog had nine puppies. He gave two to his friends.
How many puppies does he have now ?   ________

7) Benny had nine turnips in the garden. The rabbits ate two of the turnips.
How many turnips does Benny now have ?   ________

8) A restaurant made 6 salads to serve during lunch. Only 4 were
actually served. How many salads were left over from lunch ?   ________

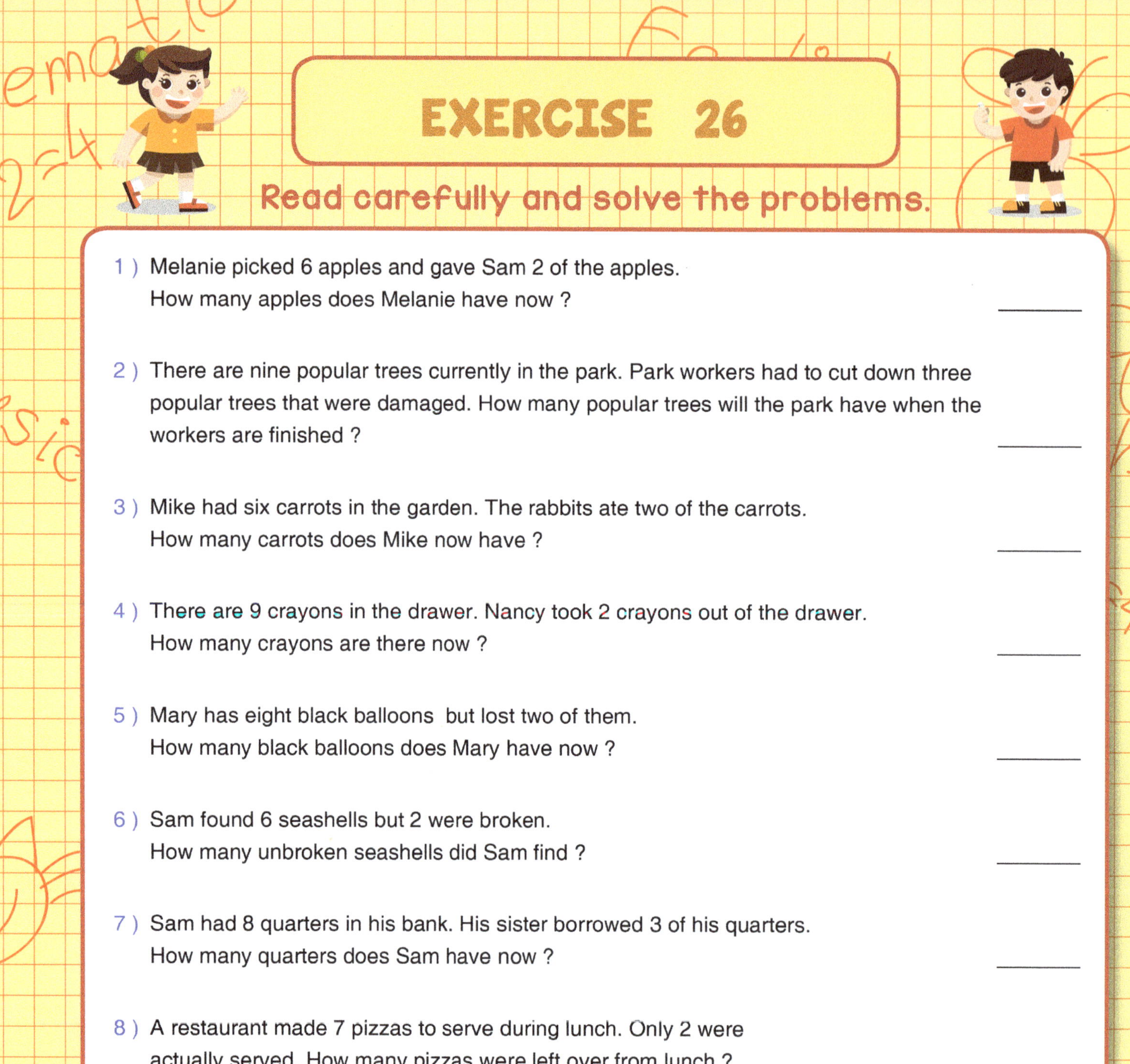

EXERCISE 26

Read carefully and solve the problems.

1) Melanie picked 6 apples and gave Sam 2 of the apples.
How many apples does Melanie have now ?   ________

2) There are nine popular trees currently in the park. Park workers had to cut down three
popular trees that were damaged. How many popular trees will the park have when the
workers are finished ?   ________

3) Mike had six carrots in the garden. The rabbits ate two of the carrots.
How many carrots does Mike now have ?   ________

4) There are 9 crayons in the drawer. Nancy took 2 crayons out of the drawer.
How many crayons are there now ?   ________

5) Mary has eight black balloons but lost two of them.
How many black balloons does Mary have now ?   ________

6) Sam found 6 seashells but 2 were broken.
How many unbroken seashells did Sam find ?   ________

7) Sam had 8 quarters in his bank. His sister borrowed 3 of his quarters.
How many quarters does Sam have now ?   ________

8) A restaurant made 7 pizzas to serve during lunch. Only 2 were
actually served. How many pizzas were left over from lunch ?   ________

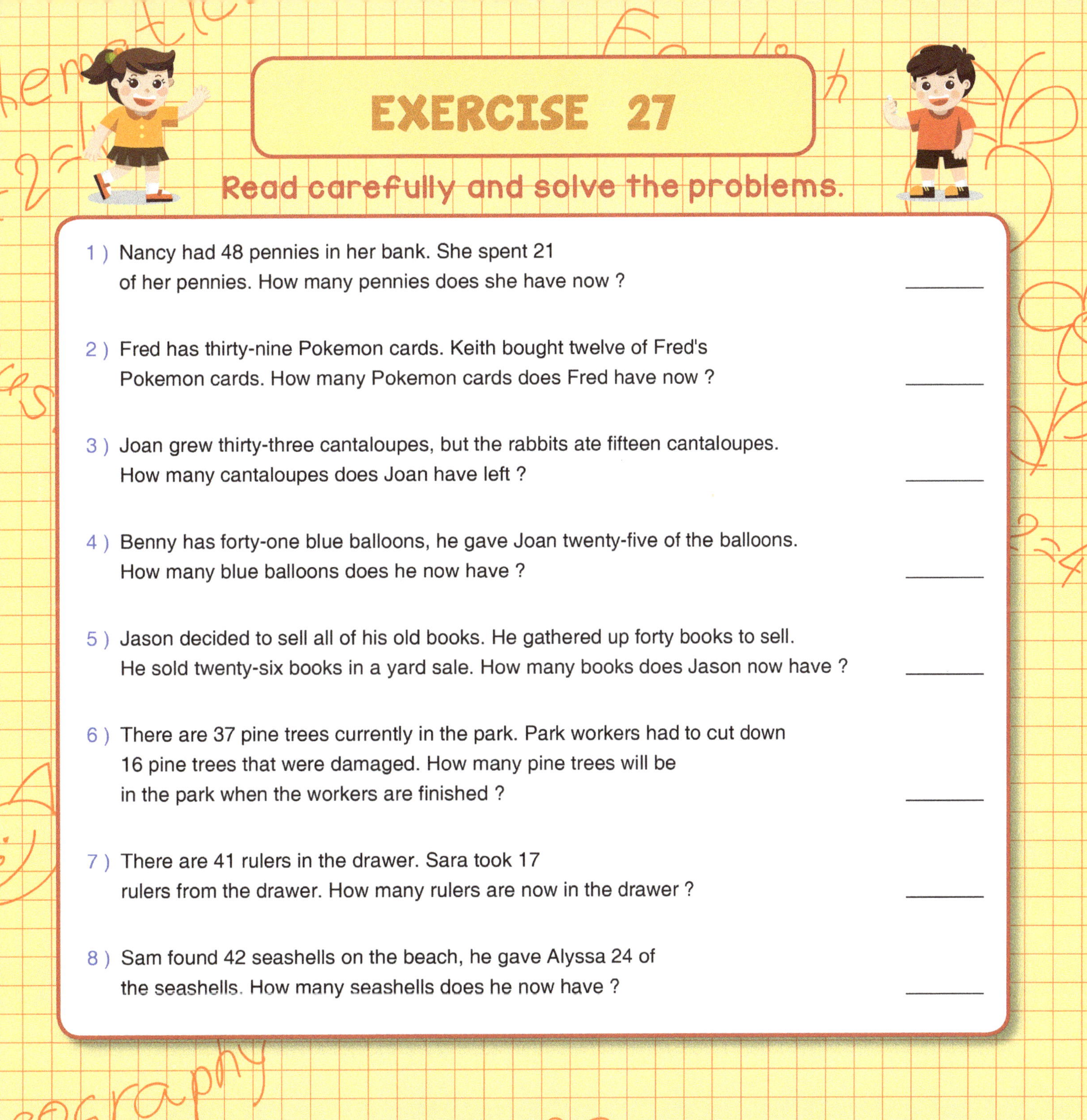

EXERCISE 27

Read carefully and solve the problems.

1) Nancy had 48 pennies in her bank. She spent 21
of her pennies. How many pennies does she have now ?　__________

2) Fred has thirty-nine Pokemon cards. Keith bought twelve of Fred's
Pokemon cards. How many Pokemon cards does Fred have now ?　__________

3) Joan grew thirty-three cantaloupes, but the rabbits ate fifteen cantaloupes.
How many cantaloupes does Joan have left ?　__________

4) Benny has forty-one blue balloons, he gave Joan twenty-five of the balloons.
How many blue balloons does he now have ?　__________

5) Jason decided to sell all of his old books. He gathered up forty books to sell.
He sold twenty-six books in a yard sale. How many books does Jason now have ?　__________

6) There are 37 pine trees currently in the park. Park workers had to cut down
16 pine trees that were damaged. How many pine trees will be
in the park when the workers are finished ?　__________

7) There are 41 rulers in the drawer. Sara took 17
rulers from the drawer. How many rulers are now in the drawer ?　__________

8) Sam found 42 seashells on the beach, he gave Alyssa 24 of
the seashells. How many seashells does he now have ?　__________

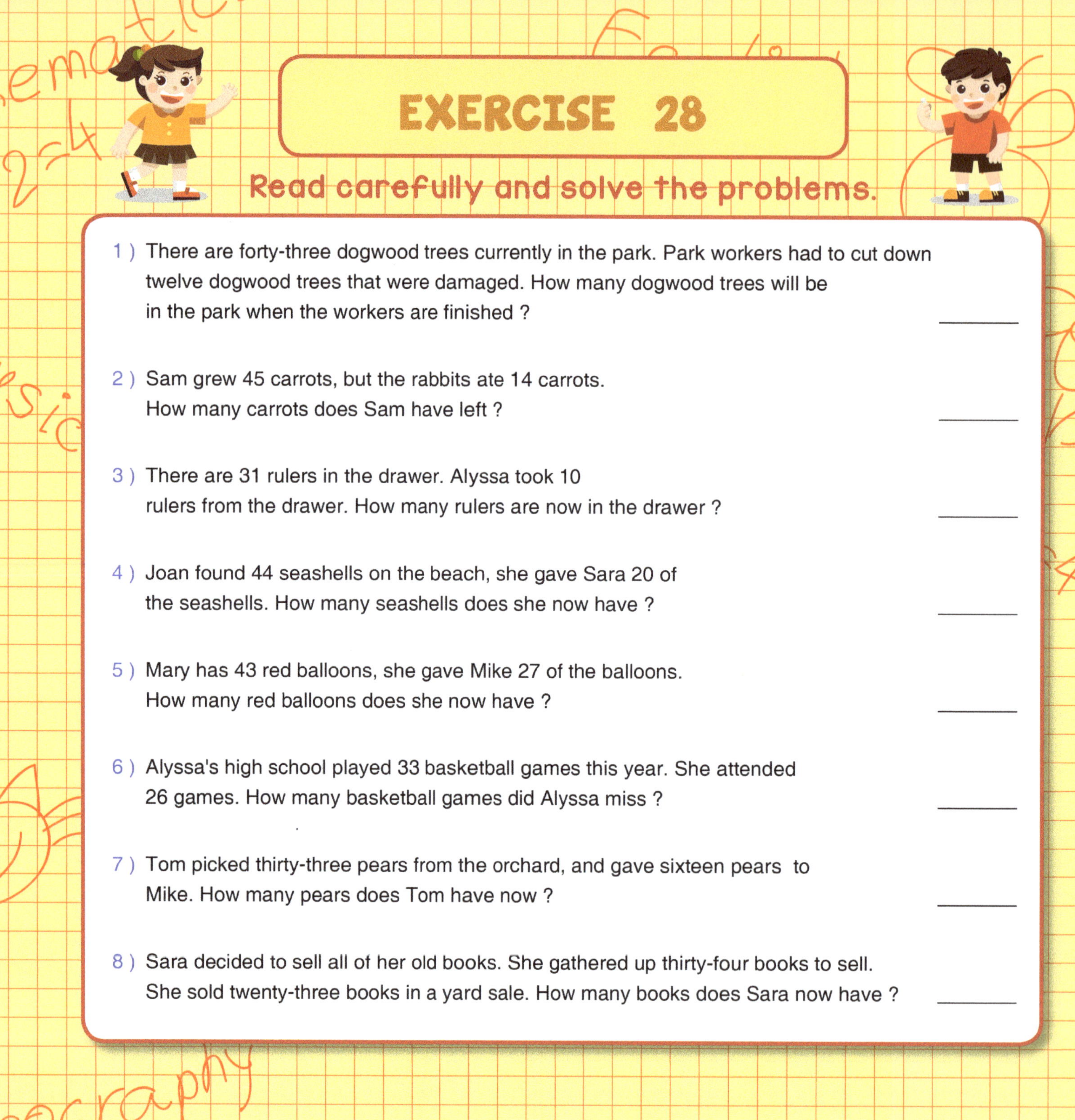

EXERCISE 28

Read carefully and solve the problems.

1) There are forty-three dogwood trees currently in the park. Park workers had to cut down twelve dogwood trees that were damaged. How many dogwood trees will be in the park when the workers are finished ? __________

2) Sam grew 45 carrots, but the rabbits ate 14 carrots. How many carrots does Sam have left ? __________

3) There are 31 rulers in the drawer. Alyssa took 10 rulers from the drawer. How many rulers are now in the drawer ? __________

4) Joan found 44 seashells on the beach, she gave Sara 20 of the seashells. How many seashells does she now have ? __________

5) Mary has 43 red balloons, she gave Mike 27 of the balloons. How many red balloons does she now have ? __________

6) Alyssa's high school played 33 basketball games this year. She attended 26 games. How many basketball games did Alyssa miss ? __________

7) Tom picked thirty-three pears from the orchard, and gave sixteen pears to Mike. How many pears does Tom have now ? __________

8) Sara decided to sell all of her old books. She gathered up thirty-four books to sell. She sold twenty-three books in a yard sale. How many books does Sara now have ? __________

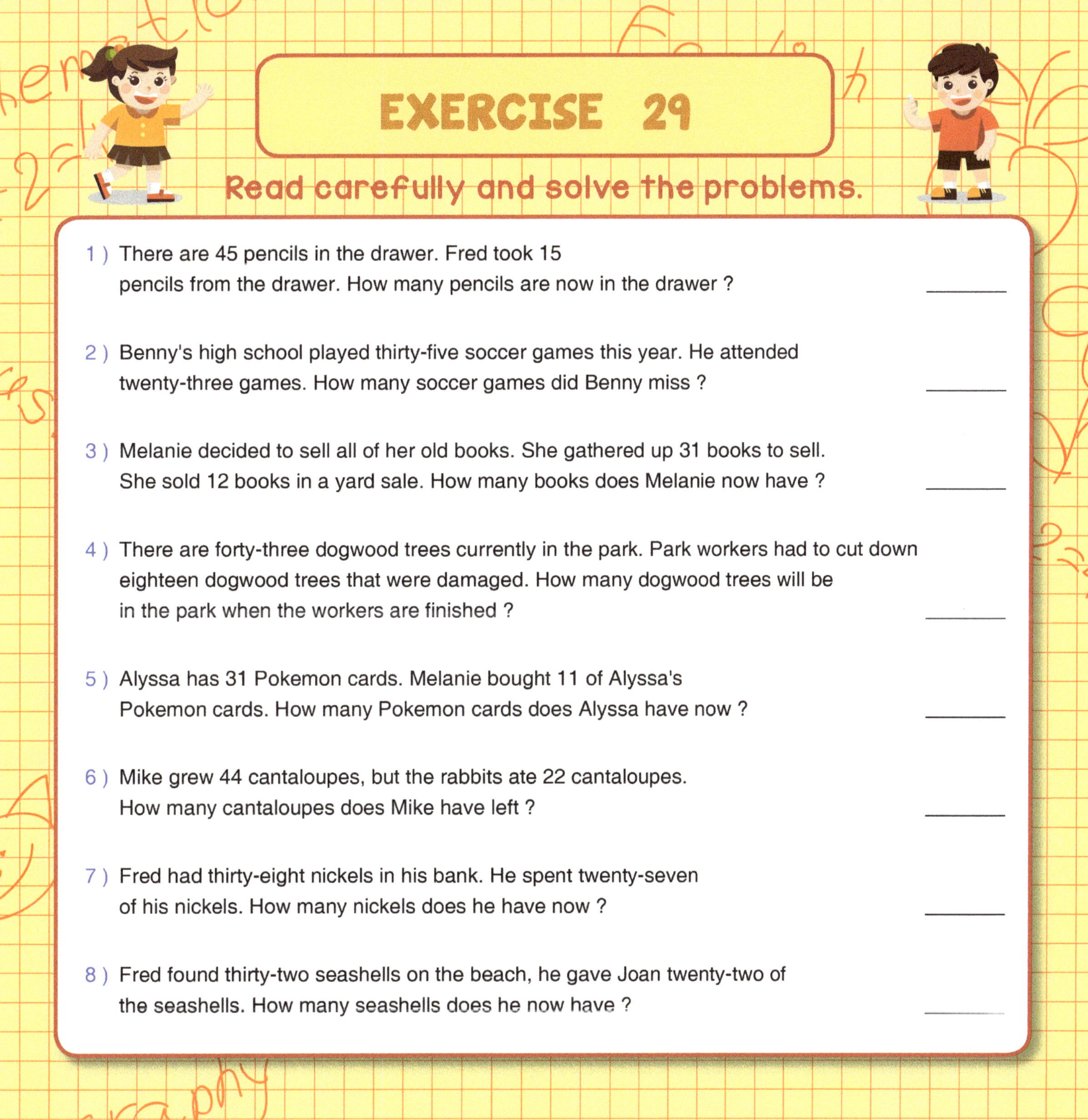

EXERCISE 29

Read carefully and solve the problems.

1) There are 45 pencils in the drawer. Fred took 15
pencils from the drawer. How many pencils are now in the drawer ?   ________

2) Benny's high school played thirty-five soccer games this year. He attended
twenty-three games. How many soccer games did Benny miss ?   ________

3) Melanie decided to sell all of her old books. She gathered up 31 books to sell.
She sold 12 books in a yard sale. How many books does Melanie now have ?   ________

4) There are forty-three dogwood trees currently in the park. Park workers had to cut down
eighteen dogwood trees that were damaged. How many dogwood trees will be
in the park when the workers are finished ?   ________

5) Alyssa has 31 Pokemon cards. Melanie bought 11 of Alyssa's
Pokemon cards. How many Pokemon cards does Alyssa have now ?   ________

6) Mike grew 44 cantaloupes, but the rabbits ate 22 cantaloupes.
How many cantaloupes does Mike have left ?   ________

7) Fred had thirty-eight nickels in his bank. He spent twenty-seven
of his nickels. How many nickels does he have now ?   ________

8) Fred found thirty-two seashells on the beach, he gave Joan twenty-two of
the seashells. How many seashells does he now have ?   ________

EXERCISE 30

Read carefully and solve the problems.

1) There are thirty-seven dogwood trees currently in the park. Park workers had to cut down twenty-six dogwood trees that were damaged. How many dogwood trees will be in the park when the workers are finished ? ________

2) Tim grew forty-nine cantaloupes, but the rabbits ate twelve cantaloupes. How many cantaloupes does Tim have left ? ________

3) Sara's high school played 36 baseball games this year. She attended 25 games. How many baseball games did Sara miss ? ________

4) Benny picked 46 apples from the orchard, and gave 26 apples to Fred. How many apples does Benny have now ? ________

5) Dan had 45 pennies in his bank. He spent 28 of his pennies. How many pennies does he have now ? ________

6) Tom has 44 baseball cards. Sara bought 10 of Tom's baseball cards. How many baseball cards does Tom have now ? ________

7) Sally found forty-nine seashells on the beach, she gave Dan twenty-four of the seashells. How many seashells does she now have ? ________

8) Sara decided to sell all of her old books. She gathered up thirty-four books to sell. She sold eleven books in a yard sale. How many books does Sara now have ? ________

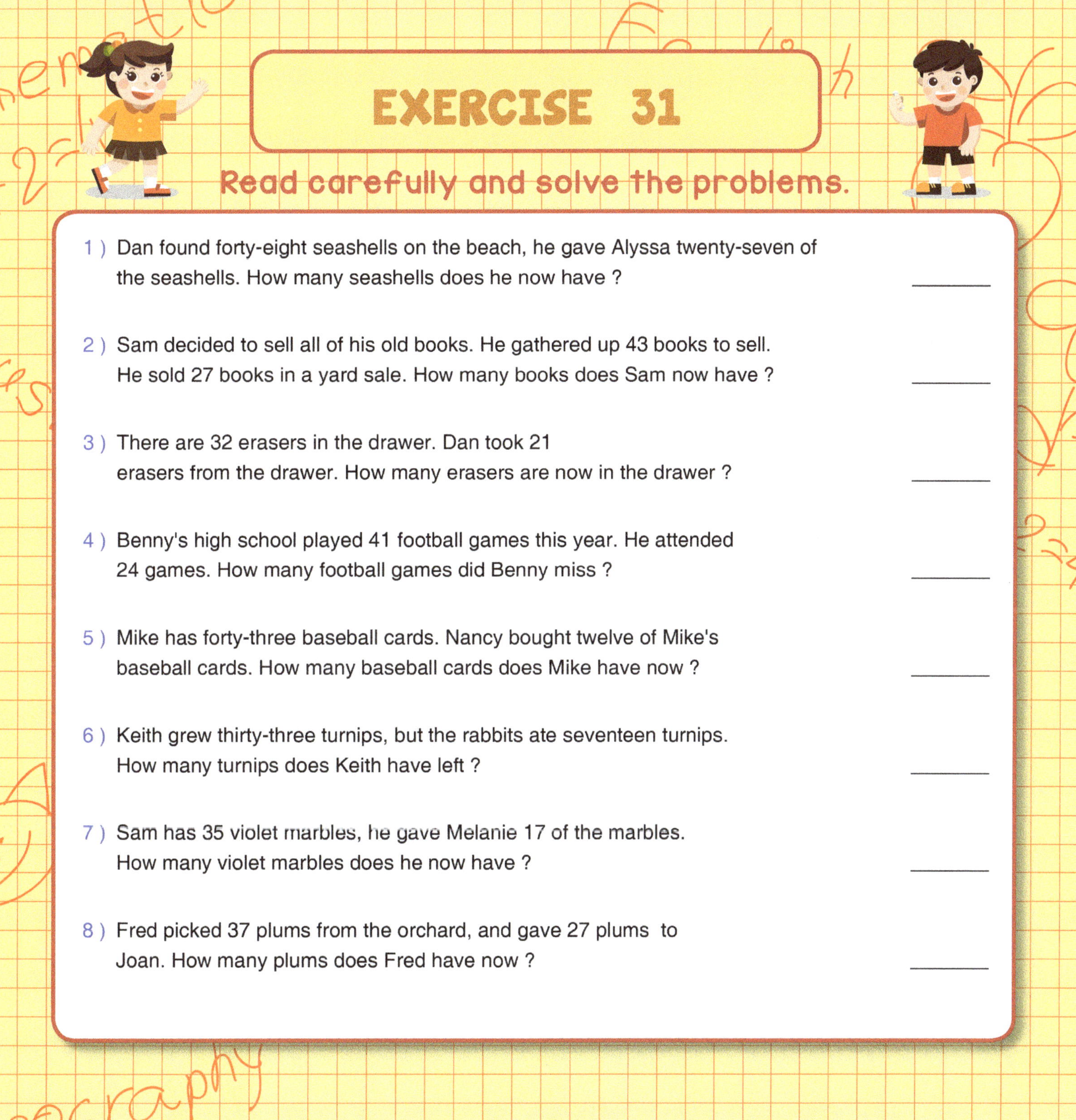

EXERCISE 31

Read carefully and solve the problems.

1) Dan found forty-eight seashells on the beach, he gave Alyssa twenty-seven of the seashells. How many seashells does he now have ? ________

2) Sam decided to sell all of his old books. He gathered up 43 books to sell. He sold 27 books in a yard sale. How many books does Sam now have ? ________

3) There are 32 erasers in the drawer. Dan took 21 erasers from the drawer. How many erasers are now in the drawer ? ________

4) Benny's high school played 41 football games this year. He attended 24 games. How many football games did Benny miss ? ________

5) Mike has forty-three baseball cards. Nancy bought twelve of Mike's baseball cards. How many baseball cards does Mike have now ? ________

6) Keith grew thirty-three turnips, but the rabbits ate seventeen turnips. How many turnips does Keith have left ? ________

7) Sam has 35 violet marbles, he gave Melanie 17 of the marbles. How many violet marbles does he now have ? ________

8) Fred picked 37 plums from the orchard, and gave 27 plums to Joan. How many plums does Fred have now ? ________

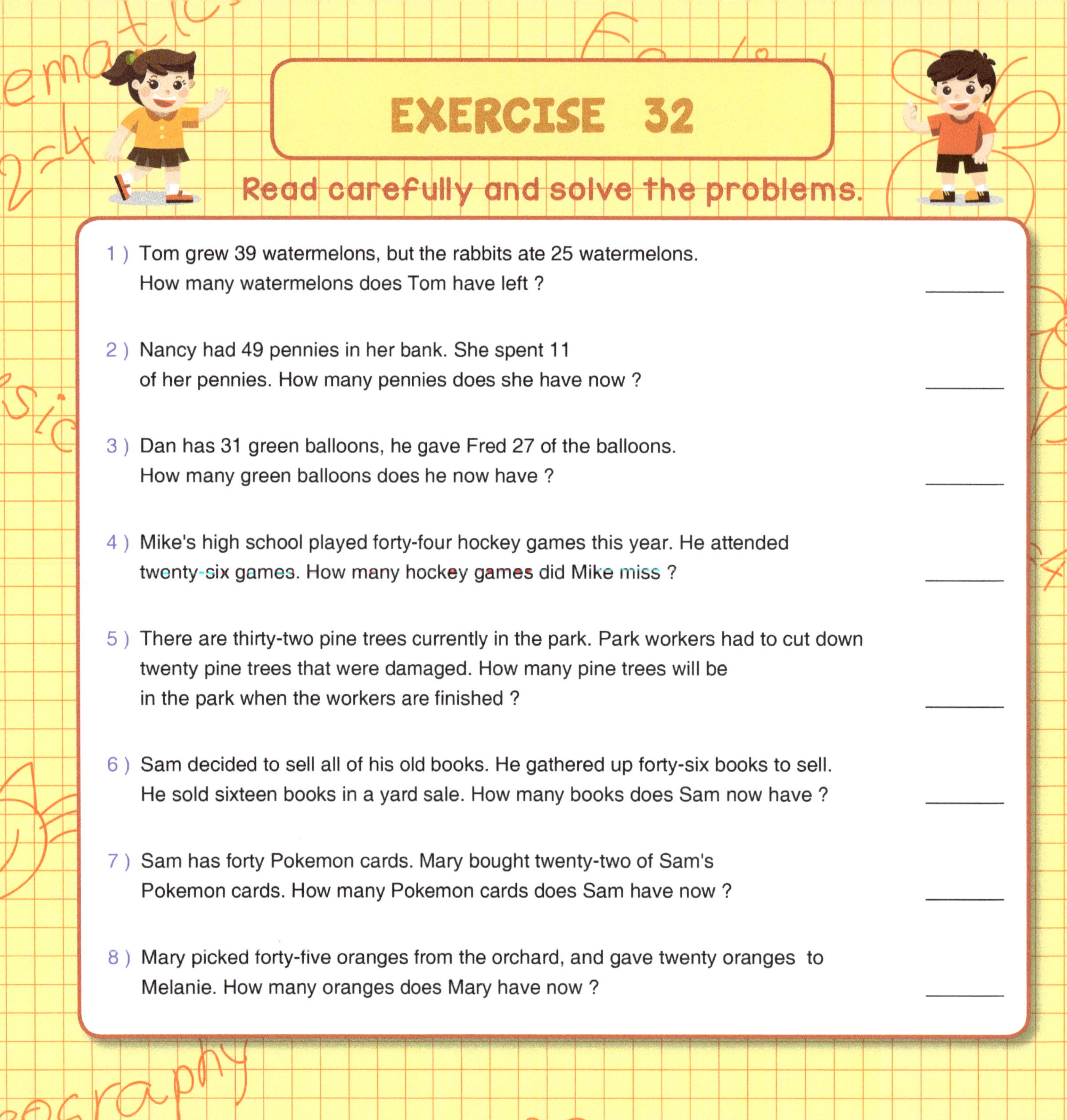

EXERCISE 32

Read carefully and solve the problems.

1) Tom grew 39 watermelons, but the rabbits ate 25 watermelons.
How many watermelons does Tom have left ?   ________

2) Nancy had 49 pennies in her bank. She spent 11
of her pennies. How many pennies does she have now ?   ________

3) Dan has 31 green balloons, he gave Fred 27 of the balloons.
How many green balloons does he now have ?   ________

4) Mike's high school played forty-four hockey games this year. He attended
twenty-six games. How many hockey games did Mike miss ?   ________

5) There are thirty-two pine trees currently in the park. Park workers had to cut down
twenty pine trees that were damaged. How many pine trees will be
in the park when the workers are finished ?   ________

6) Sam decided to sell all of his old books. He gathered up forty-six books to sell.
He sold sixteen books in a yard sale. How many books does Sam now have ?   ________

7) Sam has forty Pokemon cards. Mary bought twenty-two of Sam's
Pokemon cards. How many Pokemon cards does Sam have now ?   ________

8) Mary picked forty-five oranges from the orchard, and gave twenty oranges to
Melanie. How many oranges does Mary have now ?   ________

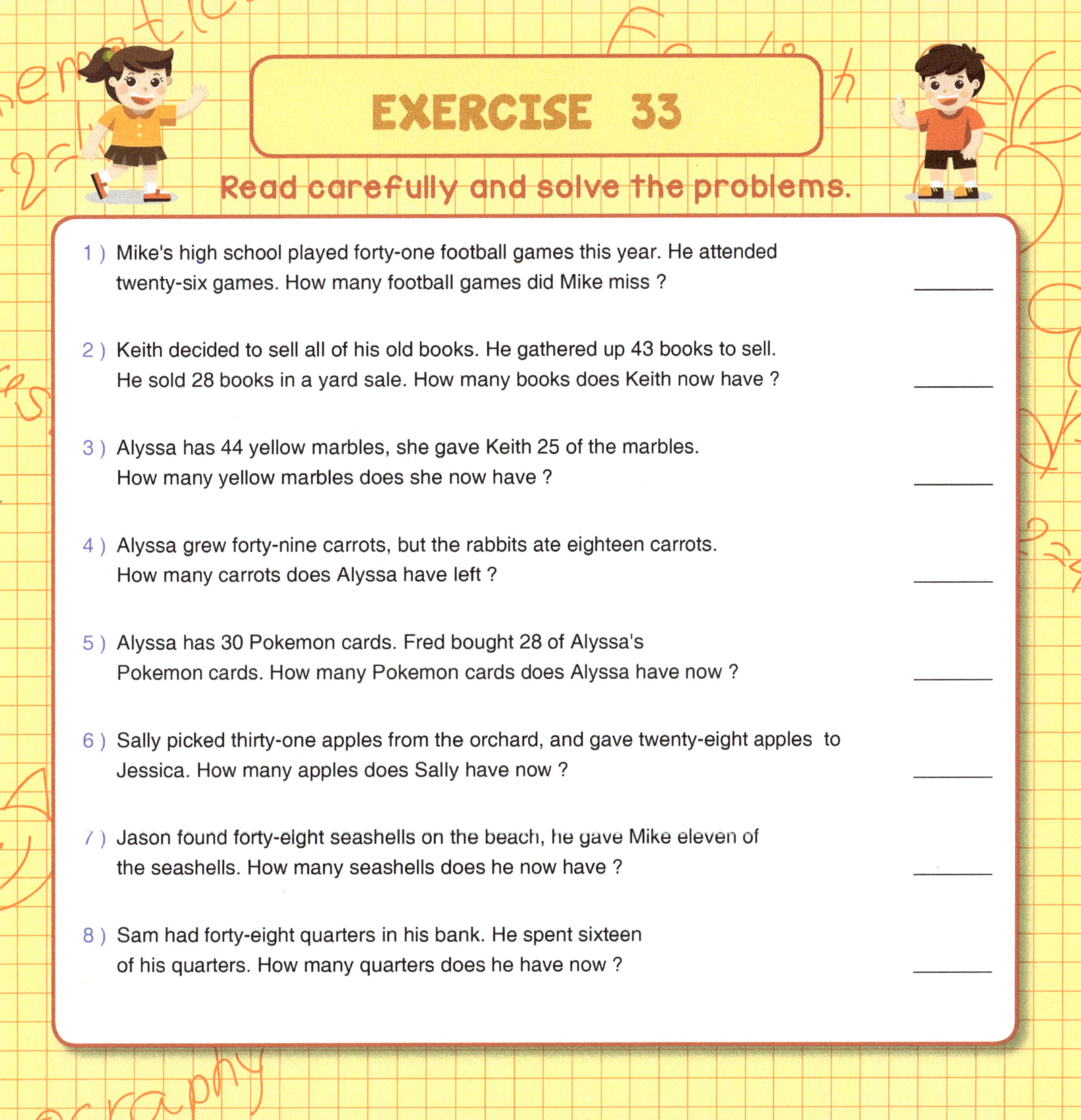

EXERCISE 33

Read carefully and solve the problems.

1) Mike's high school played forty-one football games this year. He attended twenty-six games. How many football games did Mike miss ? ________

2) Keith decided to sell all of his old books. He gathered up 43 books to sell. He sold 28 books in a yard sale. How many books does Keith now have ? ________

3) Alyssa has 44 yellow marbles, she gave Keith 25 of the marbles. How many yellow marbles does she now have ? ________

4) Alyssa grew forty-nine carrots, but the rabbits ate eighteen carrots. How many carrots does Alyssa have left ? ________

5) Alyssa has 30 Pokemon cards. Fred bought 28 of Alyssa's Pokemon cards. How many Pokemon cards does Alyssa have now ? ________

6) Sally picked thirty-one apples from the orchard, and gave twenty-eight apples to Jessica. How many apples does Sally have now ? ________

7) Jason found forty-eight seashells on the beach, he gave Mike eleven of the seashells. How many seashells does he now have ? ________

8) Sam had forty-eight quarters in his bank. He spent sixteen of his quarters. How many quarters does he have now ? ________

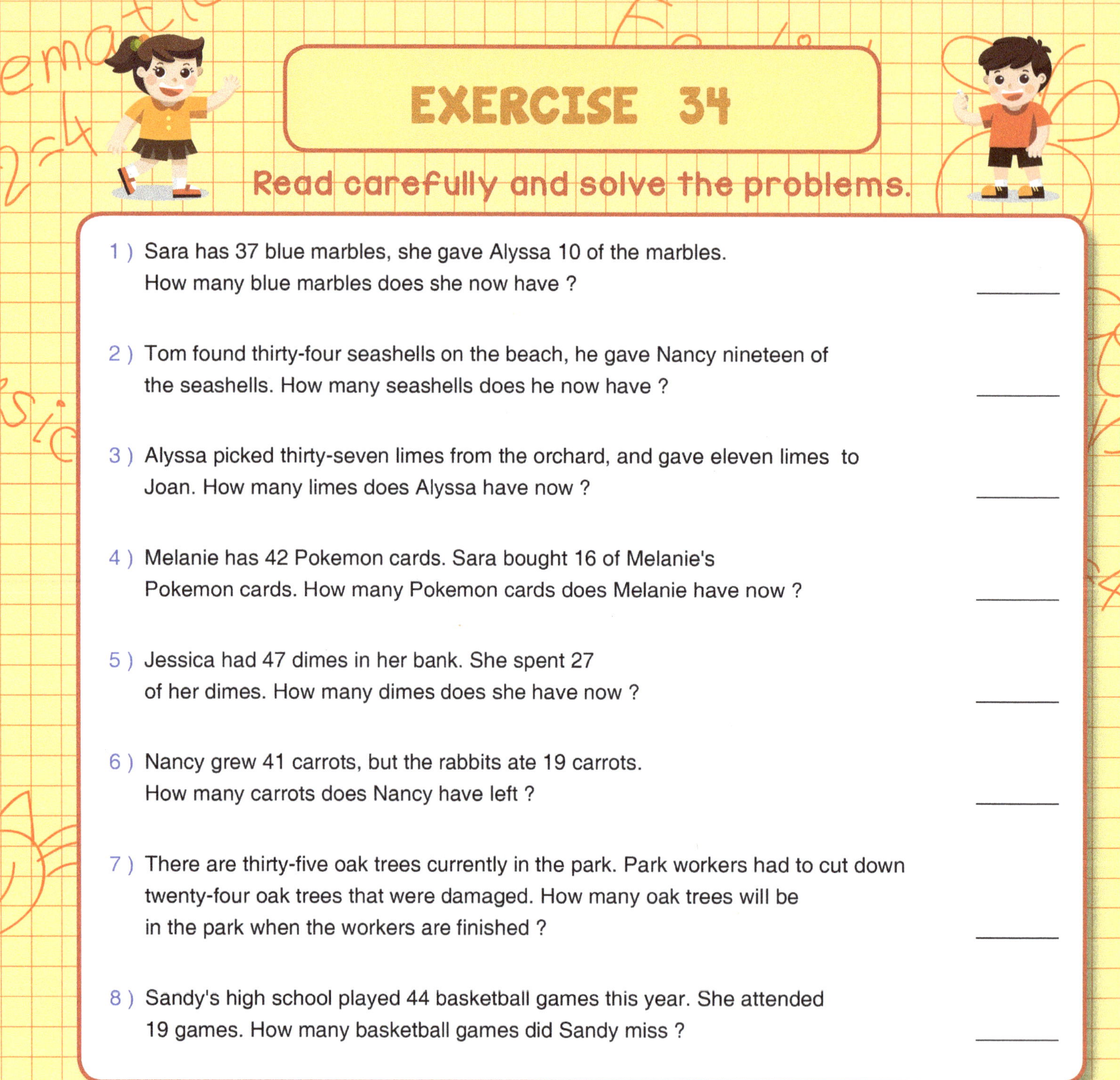

EXERCISE 34

Read carefully and solve the problems.

1) Sara has 37 blue marbles, she gave Alyssa 10 of the marbles.
How many blue marbles does she now have ? ______

2) Tom found thirty-four seashells on the beach, he gave Nancy nineteen of
the seashells. How many seashells does he now have ? ______

3) Alyssa picked thirty-seven limes from the orchard, and gave eleven limes to
Joan. How many limes does Alyssa have now ? ______

4) Melanie has 42 Pokemon cards. Sara bought 16 of Melanie's
Pokemon cards. How many Pokemon cards does Melanie have now ? ______

5) Jessica had 47 dimes in her bank. She spent 27
of her dimes. How many dimes does she have now ? ______

6) Nancy grew 41 carrots, but the rabbits ate 19 carrots.
How many carrots does Nancy have left ? ______

7) There are thirty-five oak trees currently in the park. Park workers had to cut down
twenty-four oak trees that were damaged. How many oak trees will be
in the park when the workers are finished ? ______

8) Sandy's high school played 44 basketball games this year. She attended
19 games. How many basketball games did Sandy miss ? ______

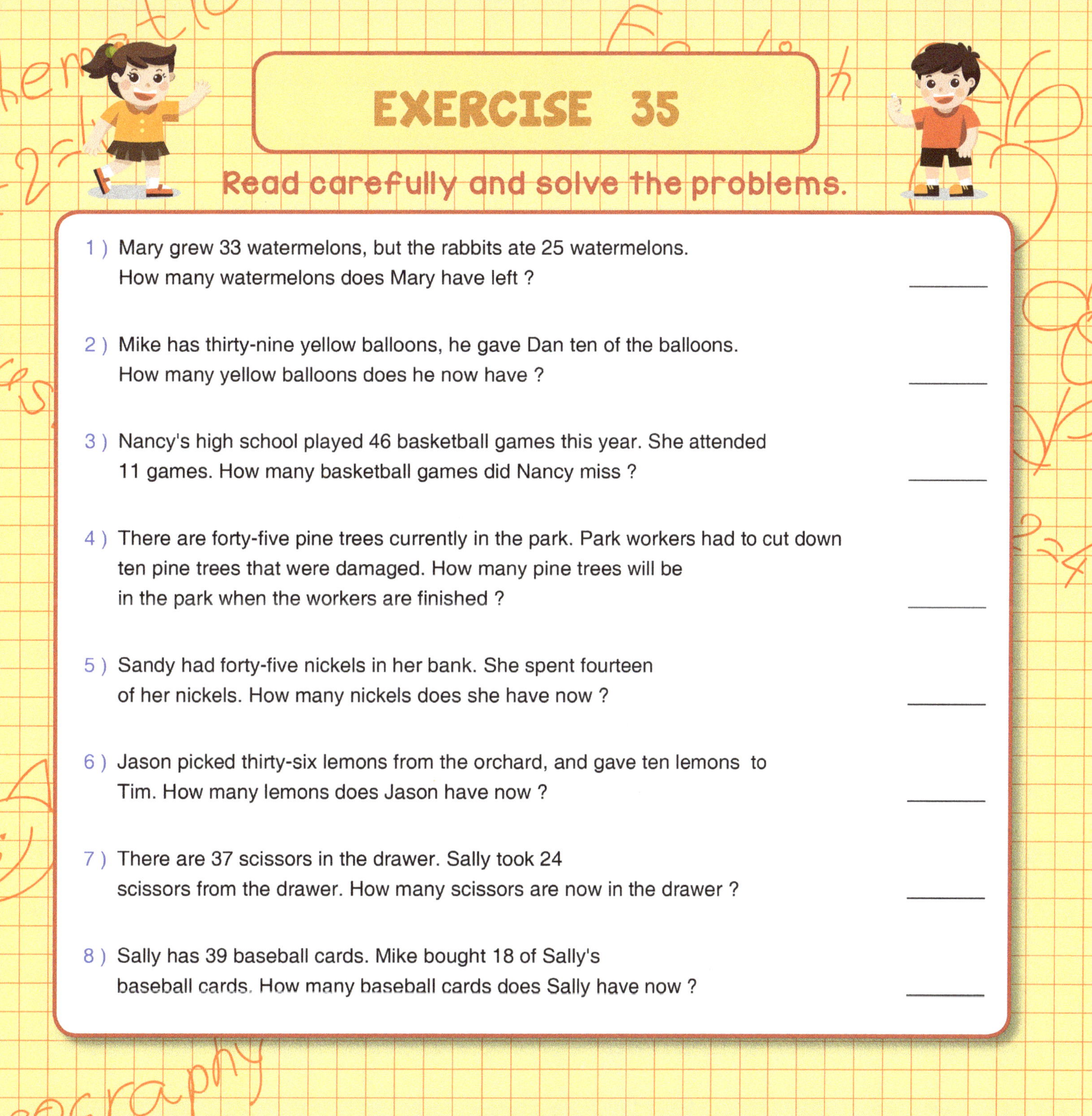

EXERCISE 35

Read carefully and solve the problems.

1) Mary grew 33 watermelons, but the rabbits ate 25 watermelons.
How many watermelons does Mary have left ? ________

2) Mike has thirty-nine yellow balloons, he gave Dan ten of the balloons.
How many yellow balloons does he now have ? ________

3) Nancy's high school played 46 basketball games this year. She attended
11 games. How many basketball games did Nancy miss ? ________

4) There are forty-five pine trees currently in the park. Park workers had to cut down
ten pine trees that were damaged. How many pine trees will be
in the park when the workers are finished ? ________

5) Sandy had forty-five nickels in her bank. She spent fourteen
of her nickels. How many nickels does she have now ? ________

6) Jason picked thirty-six lemons from the orchard, and gave ten lemons to
Tim. How many lemons does Jason have now ? ________

7) There are 37 scissors in the drawer. Sally took 24
scissors from the drawer. How many scissors are now in the drawer ? ________

8) Sally has 39 baseball cards. Mike bought 18 of Sally's
baseball cards. How many baseball cards does Sally have now ? ________

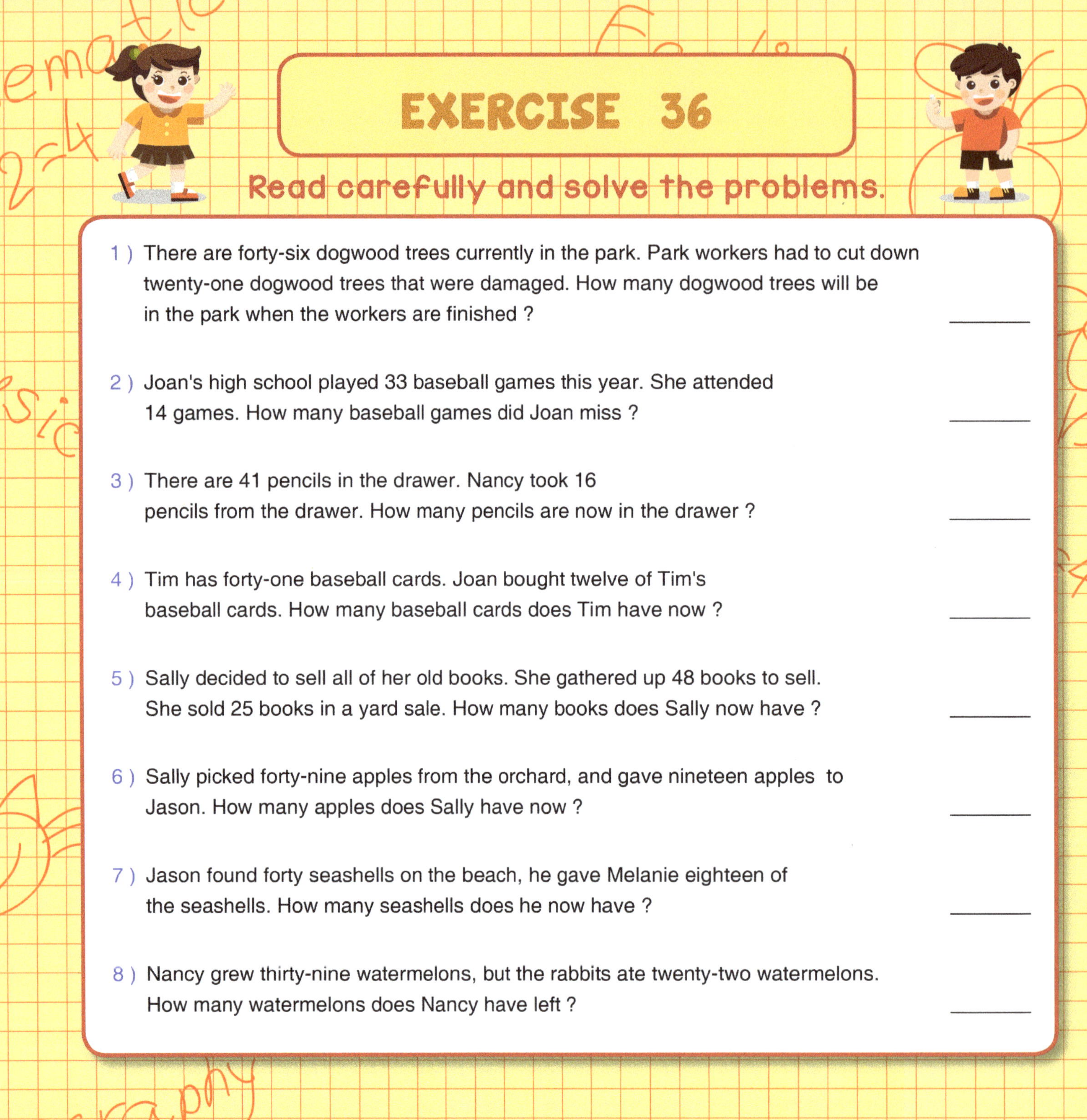

EXERCISE 36

Read carefully and solve the problems.

1) There are forty-six dogwood trees currently in the park. Park workers had to cut down twenty-one dogwood trees that were damaged. How many dogwood trees will be in the park when the workers are finished ? ________

2) Joan's high school played 33 baseball games this year. She attended 14 games. How many baseball games did Joan miss ? ________

3) There are 41 pencils in the drawer. Nancy took 16 pencils from the drawer. How many pencils are now in the drawer ? ________

4) Tim has forty-one baseball cards. Joan bought twelve of Tim's baseball cards. How many baseball cards does Tim have now ? ________

5) Sally decided to sell all of her old books. She gathered up 48 books to sell. She sold 25 books in a yard sale. How many books does Sally now have ? ________

6) Sally picked forty-nine apples from the orchard, and gave nineteen apples to Jason. How many apples does Sally have now ? ________

7) Jason found forty seashells on the beach, he gave Melanie eighteen of the seashells. How many seashells does he now have ? ________

8) Nancy grew thirty-nine watermelons, but the rabbits ate twenty-two watermelons. How many watermelons does Nancy have left ? ________

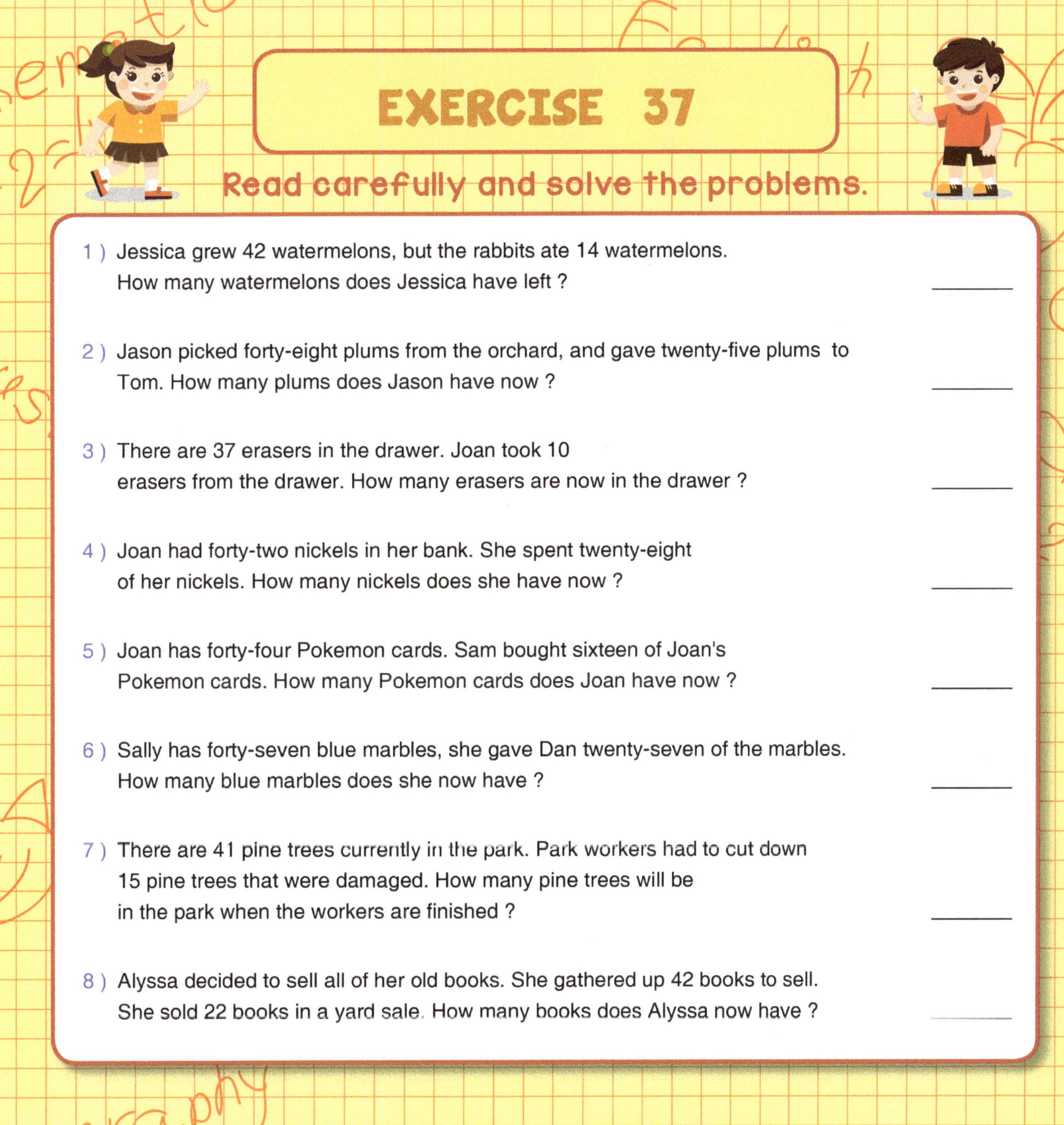

EXERCISE 37

Read carefully and solve the problems.

1) Jessica grew 42 watermelons, but the rabbits ate 14 watermelons.
How many watermelons does Jessica have left ?   ________

2) Jason picked forty-eight plums from the orchard, and gave twenty-five plums to
Tom. How many plums does Jason have now ?   ________

3) There are 37 erasers in the drawer. Joan took 10
erasers from the drawer. How many erasers are now in the drawer ?   ________

4) Joan had forty-two nickels in her bank. She spent twenty-eight
of her nickels. How many nickels does she have now ?   ________

5) Joan has forty-four Pokemon cards. Sam bought sixteen of Joan's
Pokemon cards. How many Pokemon cards does Joan have now ?   ________

6) Sally has forty-seven blue marbles, she gave Dan twenty-seven of the marbles.
How many blue marbles does she now have ?   ________

7) There are 41 pine trees currently in the park. Park workers had to cut down
15 pine trees that were damaged. How many pine trees will be
in the park when the workers are finished ?   ________

8) Alyssa decided to sell all of her old books. She gathered up 42 books to sell.
She sold 22 books in a yard sale. How many books does Alyssa now have ?   ________

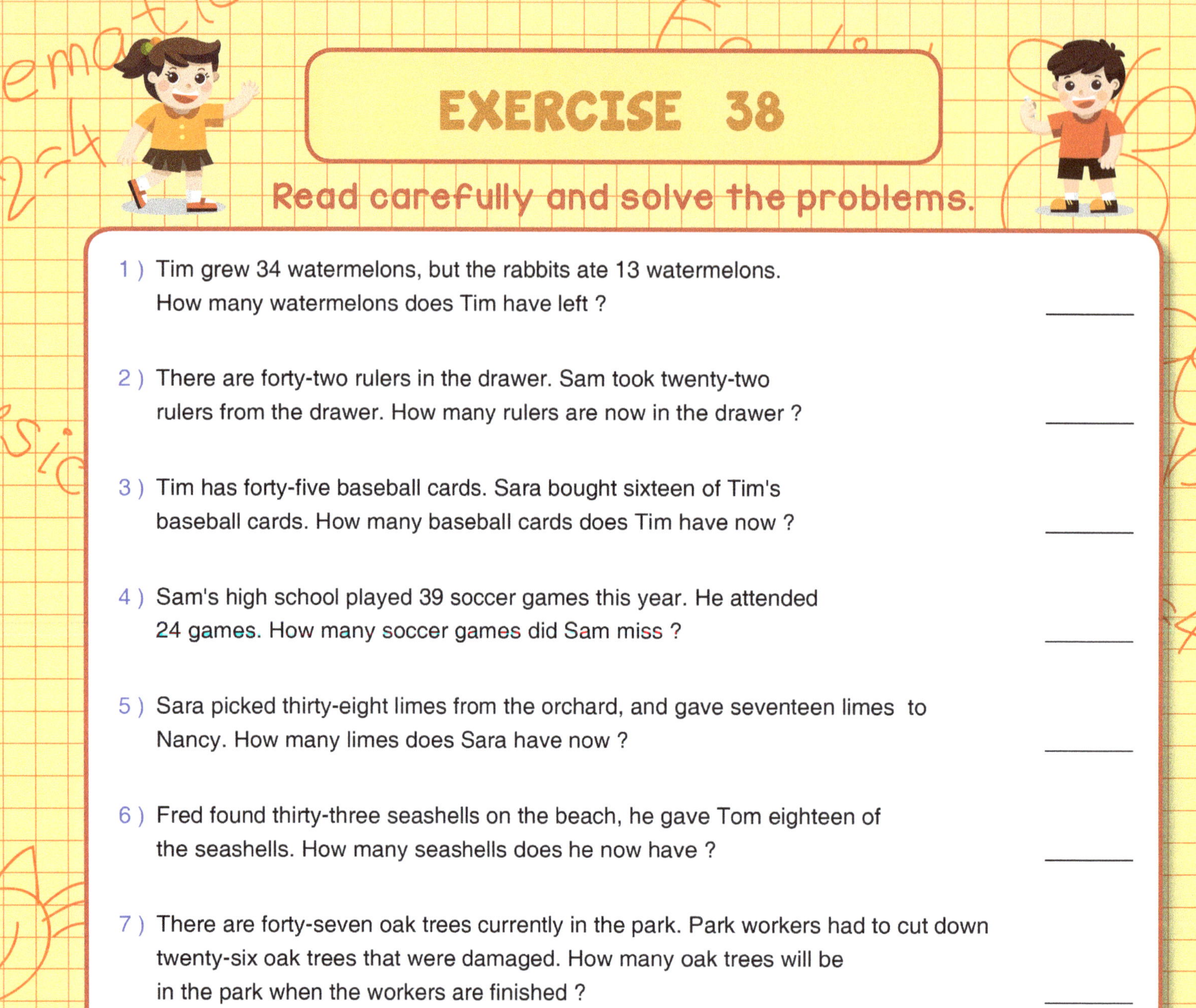

EXERCISE 38

Read carefully and solve the problems.

1) Tim grew 34 watermelons, but the rabbits ate 13 watermelons.
How many watermelons does Tim have left ? ________

2) There are forty-two rulers in the drawer. Sam took twenty-two
rulers from the drawer. How many rulers are now in the drawer ? ________

3) Tim has forty-five baseball cards. Sara bought sixteen of Tim's
baseball cards. How many baseball cards does Tim have now ? ________

4) Sam's high school played 39 soccer games this year. He attended
24 games. How many soccer games did Sam miss ? ________

5) Sara picked thirty-eight limes from the orchard, and gave seventeen limes to
Nancy. How many limes does Sara have now ? ________

6) Fred found thirty-three seashells on the beach, he gave Tom eighteen of
the seashells. How many seashells does he now have ? ________

7) There are forty-seven oak trees currently in the park. Park workers had to cut down
twenty-six oak trees that were damaged. How many oak trees will be
in the park when the workers are finished ? ________

8) Sara had 47 dimes in her bank. She spent 25
of her dimes. How many dimes does she have now ? ________

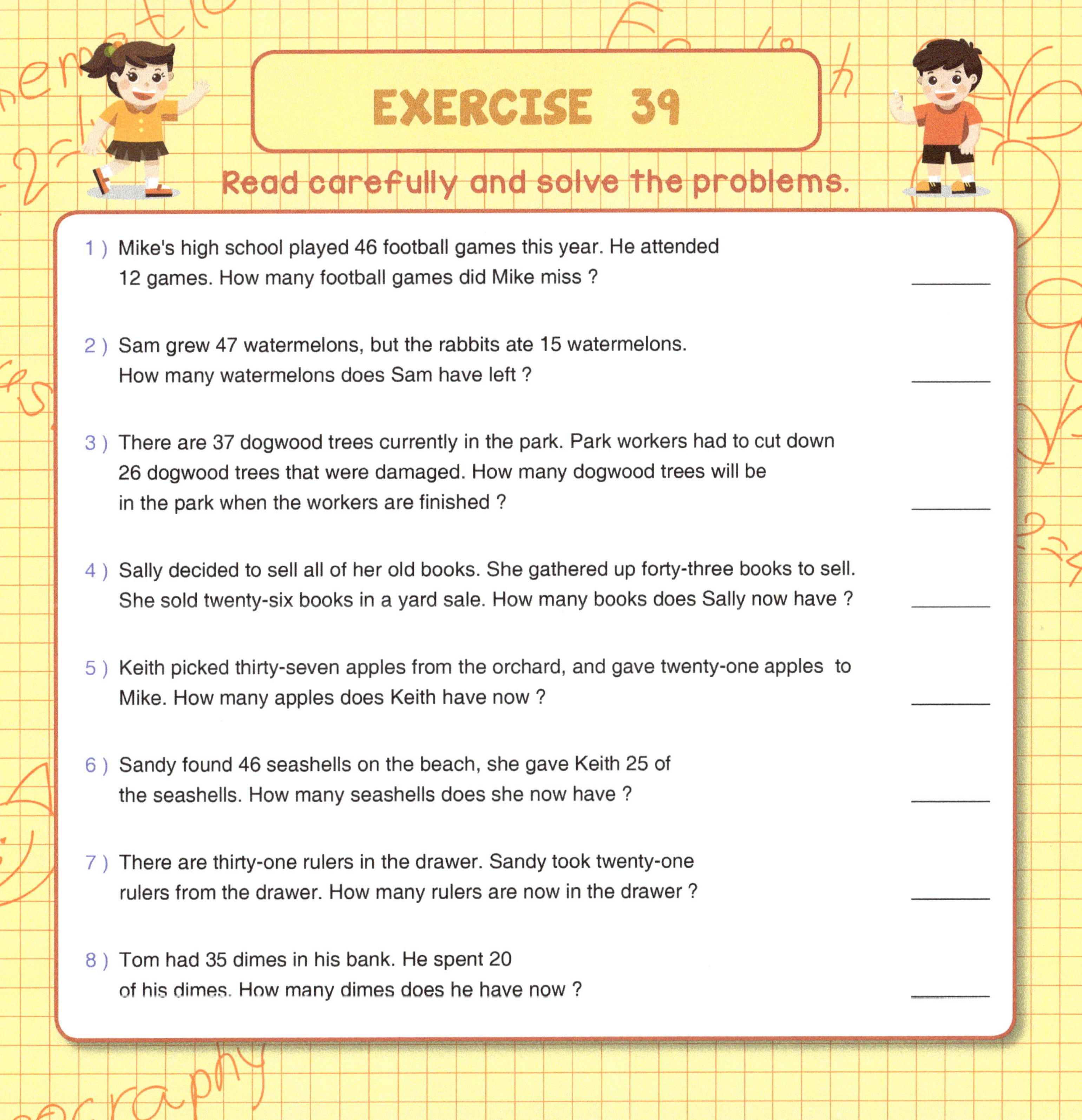

EXERCISE 39

Read carefully and solve the problems.

1) Mike's high school played 46 football games this year. He attended
12 games. How many football games did Mike miss ?   ________

2) Sam grew 47 watermelons, but the rabbits ate 15 watermelons.
How many watermelons does Sam have left ?   ________

3) There are 37 dogwood trees currently in the park. Park workers had to cut down
26 dogwood trees that were damaged. How many dogwood trees will be
in the park when the workers are finished ?   ________

4) Sally decided to sell all of her old books. She gathered up forty-three books to sell.
She sold twenty-six books in a yard sale. How many books does Sally now have ?   ________

5) Keith picked thirty-seven apples from the orchard, and gave twenty-one apples to
Mike. How many apples does Keith have now ?   ________

6) Sandy found 46 seashells on the beach, she gave Keith 25 of
the seashells. How many seashells does she now have ?   ________

7) There are thirty-one rulers in the drawer. Sandy took twenty-one
rulers from the drawer. How many rulers are now in the drawer ?   ________

8) Tom had 35 dimes in his bank. He spent 20
of his dimes. How many dimes does he have now ?   ________

EXERCISE 40

Read carefully and solve the problems.

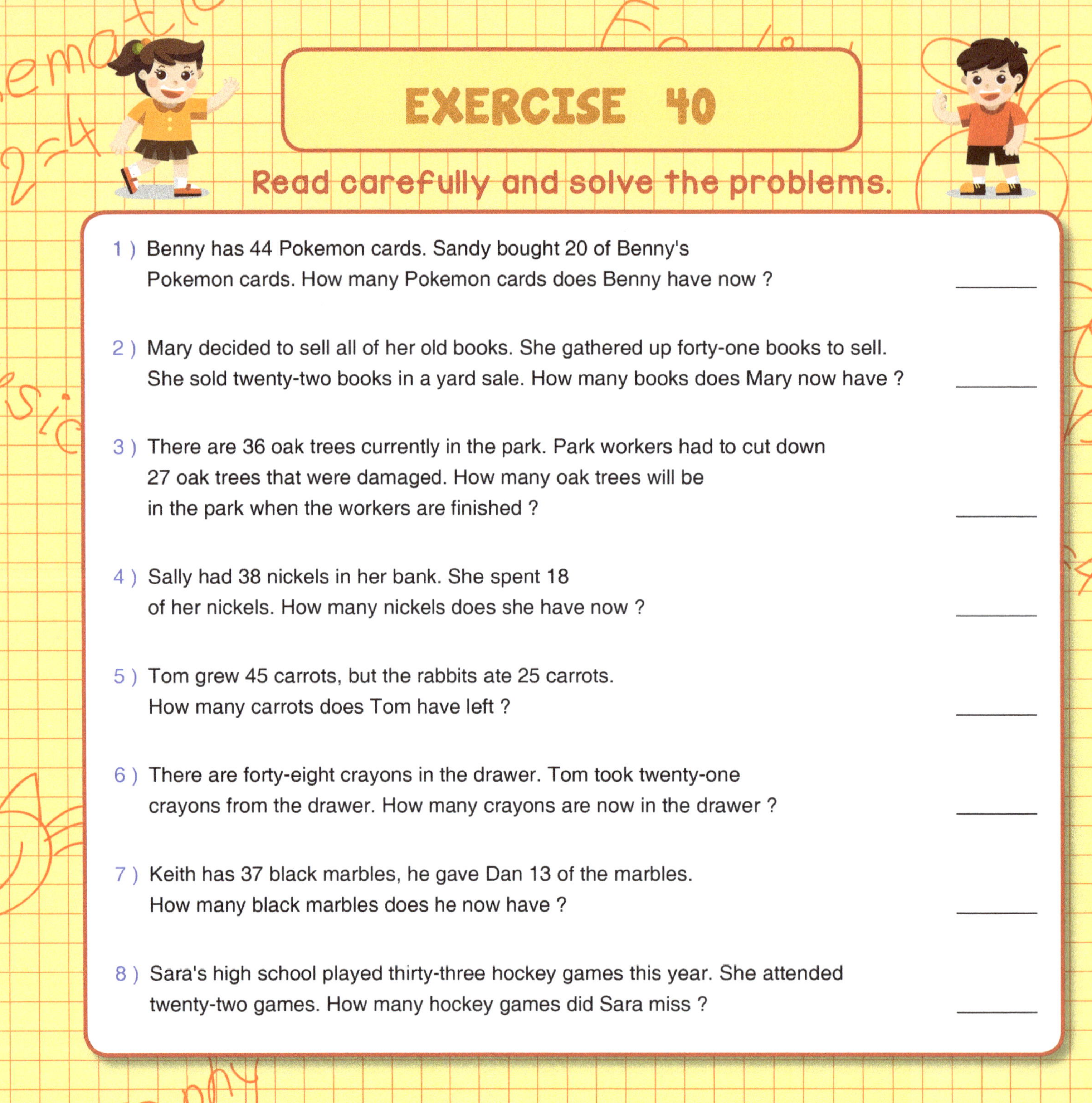

1) Benny has 44 Pokemon cards. Sandy bought 20 of Benny's
Pokemon cards. How many Pokemon cards does Benny have now ?   ________

2) Mary decided to sell all of her old books. She gathered up forty-one books to sell.
She sold twenty-two books in a yard sale. How many books does Mary now have ?   ________

3) There are 36 oak trees currently in the park. Park workers had to cut down
27 oak trees that were damaged. How many oak trees will be
in the park when the workers are finished ?   ________

4) Sally had 38 nickels in her bank. She spent 18
of her nickels. How many nickels does she have now ?   ________

5) Tom grew 45 carrots, but the rabbits ate 25 carrots.
How many carrots does Tom have left ?   ________

6) There are forty-eight crayons in the drawer. Tom took twenty-one
crayons from the drawer. How many crayons are now in the drawer ?   ________

7) Keith has 37 black marbles, he gave Dan 13 of the marbles.
How many black marbles does he now have ?   ________

8) Sara's high school played thirty-three hockey games this year. She attended
twenty-two games. How many hockey games did Sara miss ?   ________

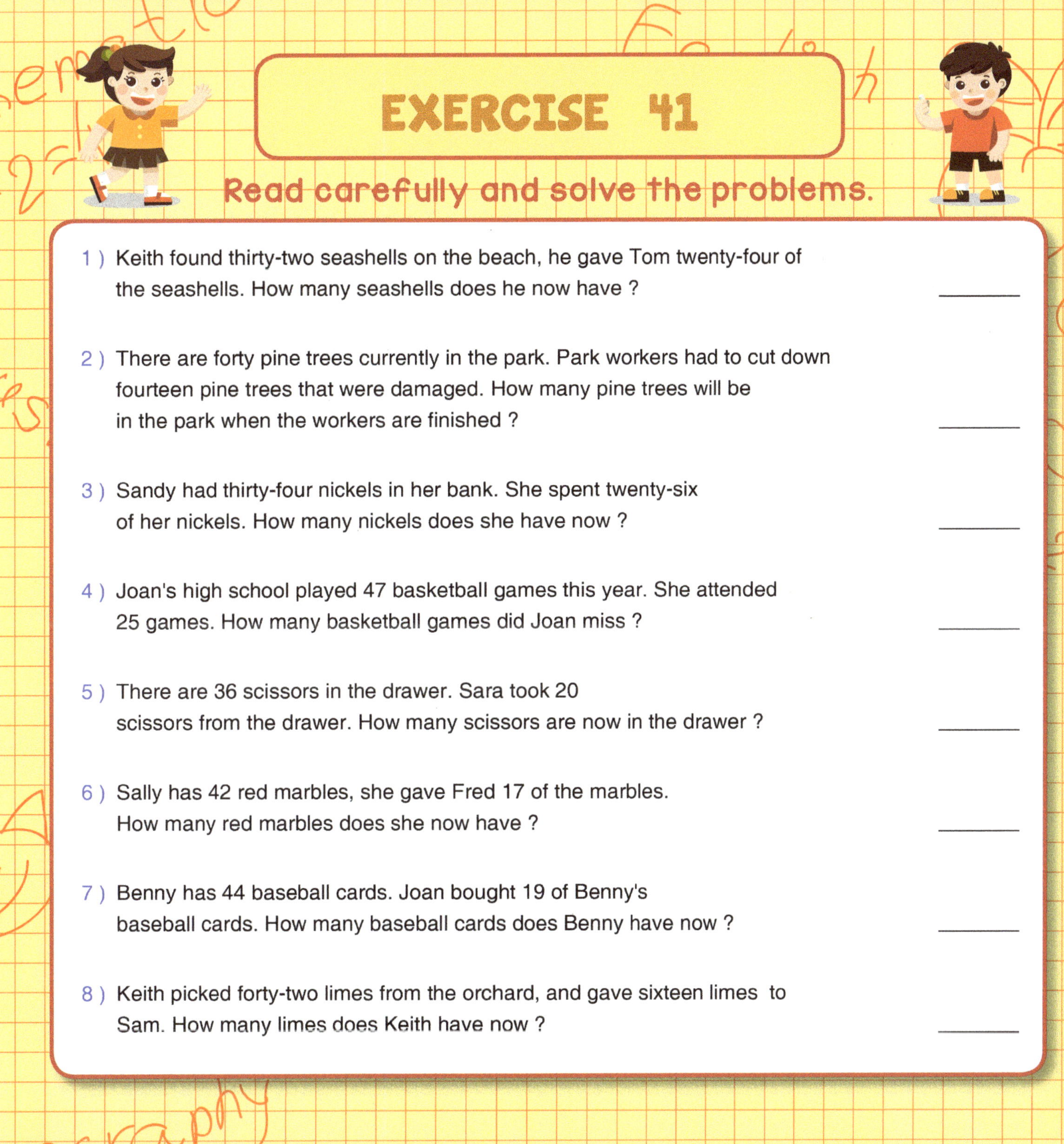

EXERCISE 41

Read carefully and solve the problems.

1) Keith found thirty-two seashells on the beach, he gave Tom twenty-four of
the seashells. How many seashells does he now have ? ________

2) There are forty pine trees currently in the park. Park workers had to cut down
fourteen pine trees that were damaged. How many pine trees will be
in the park when the workers are finished ? ________

3) Sandy had thirty-four nickels in her bank. She spent twenty-six
of her nickels. How many nickels does she have now ? ________

4) Joan's high school played 47 basketball games this year. She attended
25 games. How many basketball games did Joan miss ? ________

5) There are 36 scissors in the drawer. Sara took 20
scissors from the drawer. How many scissors are now in the drawer ? ________

6) Sally has 42 red marbles, she gave Fred 17 of the marbles.
How many red marbles does she now have ? ________

7) Benny has 44 baseball cards. Joan bought 19 of Benny's
baseball cards. How many baseball cards does Benny have now ? ________

8) Keith picked forty-two limes from the orchard, and gave sixteen limes to
Sam. How many limes does Keith have now ? ________

1) Mike decided to sell all of his old books. He gathered up forty-three books to sell.
He sold twenty-five books in a yard sale. How many books does Mike now have ? ________

2) Sara had 30 nickels in her bank. She spent 25
of her nickels. How many nickels does she have now ? ________

3) There are thirty-nine rulers in the drawer. Tom took twenty-seven
rulers from the drawer. How many rulers are now in the drawer ? ________

4) There are thirty-nine popular trees currently in the park. Park workers had to cut down
ten popular trees that were damaged. How many popular trees will be
in the park when the workers are finished ? ________

5) Keith's high school played 30 baseball games this year. He attended
15 games. How many baseball games did Keith miss ? ________

6) Joan found 39 seashells on the beach, she gave Jessica 22 of
the seashells. How many seashells does she now have ? ________

7) Joan grew 30 cantaloupes, but the rabbits ate 21 cantaloupes.
How many cantaloupes does Joan have left ? ________

8) Sally has 47 Pokemon cards. Mary bought 13 of Sally's
Pokemon cards. How many Pokemon cards does Sally have now ? ________

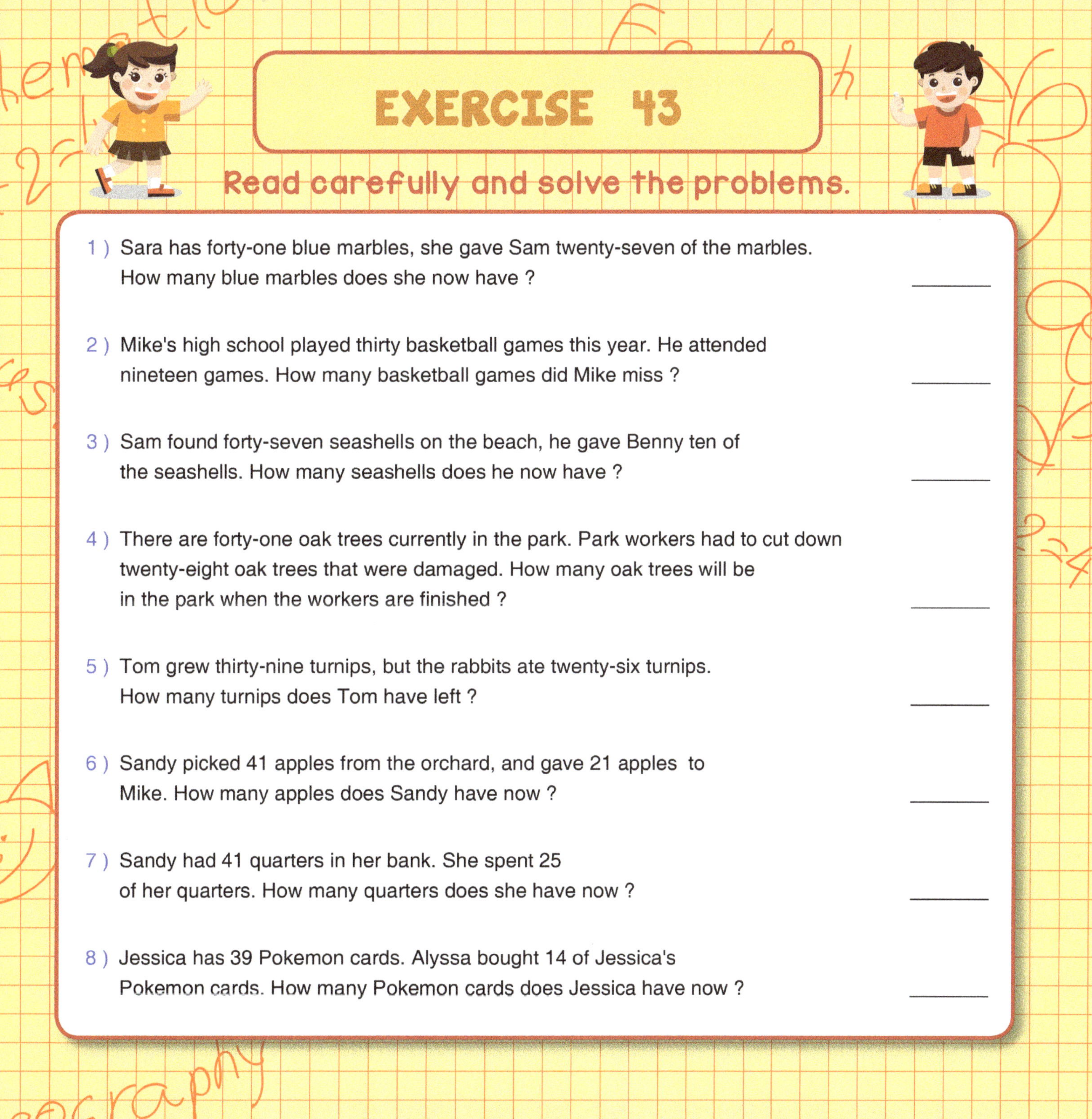

EXERCISE 43

Read carefully and solve the problems.

1) Sara has forty-one blue marbles, she gave Sam twenty-seven of the marbles. How many blue marbles does she now have ? ________

2) Mike's high school played thirty basketball games this year. He attended nineteen games. How many basketball games did Mike miss ? ________

3) Sam found forty-seven seashells on the beach, he gave Benny ten of the seashells. How many seashells does he now have ? ________

4) There are forty-one oak trees currently in the park. Park workers had to cut down twenty-eight oak trees that were damaged. How many oak trees will be in the park when the workers are finished ? ________

5) Tom grew thirty-nine turnips, but the rabbits ate twenty-six turnips. How many turnips does Tom have left ? ________

6) Sandy picked 41 apples from the orchard, and gave 21 apples to Mike. How many apples does Sandy have now ? ________

7) Sandy had 41 quarters in her bank. She spent 25 of her quarters. How many quarters does she have now ? ________

8) Jessica has 39 Pokemon cards. Alyssa bought 14 of Jessica's Pokemon cards. How many Pokemon cards does Jessica have now ? ________

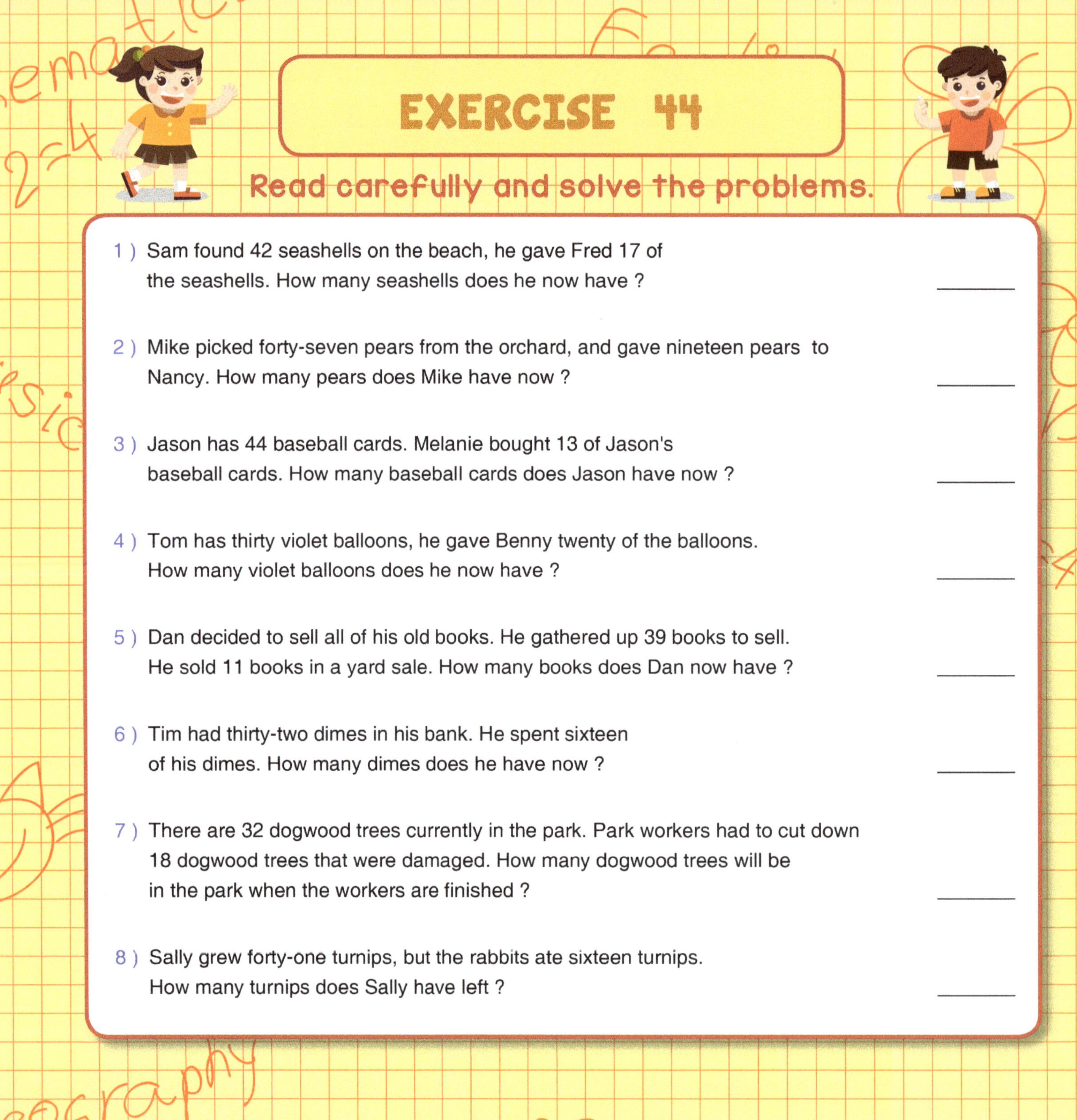

EXERCISE 44

Read carefully and solve the problems.

1) Sam found 42 seashells on the beach, he gave Fred 17 of
the seashells. How many seashells does he now have ? ________

2) Mike picked forty-seven pears from the orchard, and gave nineteen pears to
Nancy. How many pears does Mike have now ? ________

3) Jason has 44 baseball cards. Melanie bought 13 of Jason's
baseball cards. How many baseball cards does Jason have now ? ________

4) Tom has thirty violet balloons, he gave Benny twenty of the balloons.
How many violet balloons does he now have ? ________

5) Dan decided to sell all of his old books. He gathered up 39 books to sell.
He sold 11 books in a yard sale. How many books does Dan now have ? ________

6) Tim had thirty-two dimes in his bank. He spent sixteen
of his dimes. How many dimes does he have now ? ________

7) There are 32 dogwood trees currently in the park. Park workers had to cut down
18 dogwood trees that were damaged. How many dogwood trees will be
in the park when the workers are finished ? ________

8) Sally grew forty-one turnips, but the rabbits ate sixteen turnips.
How many turnips does Sally have left ? ________

GOOD
JOB

ANSWERS!

EXERCISE 1	EXERCISE 2	EXERCISE 3	EXERCISE 4
17 hamburgers	11 hamburgers	15 pencils	13 kittens
13 violet balloons	11 red marbles	7 maple trees	10 seashells
7 kittens	13 games	12 seashells	10 yellow balloons
9 crayons	8 seashells	14 puppies	16 pears
11 games	10 nickels	17 turnips	9 quarters
6 seashells	14 oak trees	5 plums	15 watermelons
12 watermelons	11 kittens	15 games	10 rulers
9 rose bushes	15 crayons	9 black balloons	9 games

EXERCISE 5	EXERCISE 6	EXERCISE 7	EXERCISE 8
10 seashells	5 hamburgers	13 games	10 seashells
9 pine trees	8 orange marbles	16 apples	14 sandwiches
11 slices of pie	7 games	11 kittens	15 erasers
12 games	17 nickels	17 cantaloupes	13 dimes
12 yellow marbles	11 pine trees	9 seashells	11 games
14 watermelons	14 plums	15 dimes	12 maple trees
15 pennies	14 puppies	13 oak trees	9 plums
14 kittens	10 rulers	15 red marbles	17 carrots

EXERCISE 9	EXERCISE 10	EXERCISE 11	EXERCISE 12
7 watermelons	12 seashells	18 pencils	21 hot dogs
6 seashells	12 dimes	9 puppies	15 red balloons
13 poplar trees	9 scissors	13 red marbles	17 games
12 blue balloons	15 black marbles	21 onions	16 puppies
11 rulers	15 pizzas	17 seashells	15 pencils
11 quarters	13 puppies	16 salads	16 oranges
11 games	9 carrots	14 apples	17 nickels
11 plums	7 oak trees	18 games	18 pumpkins

EXERCISE 13	EXERCISE 14	EXERCISE 15	EXERCISE 16
9 games	21 pencils	15 dogwood trees	18 games
14 dimes	15 games	18 quarters	18 pears
17 pumpkins	22 pennies	17 puppies	15 violet marbles
13 blue balloons	24 lemons	17 scissors	21 oak trees
22 pine trees	13 maple trees	19 orange marbles	16 kittens
24 plums	21 kittens	17 carrots	15 onions
14 puppies	16 onions	12 pies	15 seashells
22 crayons	18 seashells	20 seashells	24 pizzas

EXERCISE 17	EXERCISE 18	EXERCISE 19	EXERCISE 20
68 blue marbles	76 dogwood trees	69 apples	33 apples
33 Pokemon cards	63 books	46 pumpkins	40 seashells
44 pencils	71 games	46 dimes	26 nickels
50 oak trees	83 baseball cards	33 Pokemon cards	67 games
36 games	36 quarters	76 books	64 pencils
72 seashells	79 yellow balloons	40 poplar trees	57 rose bushes
50 apples	65 cantaloupes	94 games	58 blue balloons
81 watermelons	56 pears	68 red marbles	85 Pokemon cards

<table>
<tr><td>**EXERCISE 21**</td><td>**EXERCISE 22**</td><td>**EXERCISE 23**</td><td>**EXERCISE 24**</td></tr>
<tr><td>2 pennies</td><td>5 pencils</td><td>3 blue balloons</td><td>3 seashells</td></tr>
<tr><td>5 pears</td><td>4 orange balloons</td><td>3 games</td><td>3 games</td></tr>
<tr><td>4 dogwood trees</td><td>4 seashells</td><td>4 erasers</td><td>4 pumpkins</td></tr>
<tr><td>3 erasers</td><td>4 cakes</td><td>5 potatoes</td><td>6 black balloons</td></tr>
<tr><td>2 black balloons</td><td>4 kittens</td><td>3 walnut trees</td><td>4 scissors</td></tr>
<tr><td>2 seashells</td><td>7 carrots</td><td>3 apples</td><td>4 kittens</td></tr>
<tr><td>6 turnips</td><td>5 rose bushes</td><td>5 puppies</td><td>4 nickels</td></tr>
<tr><td>3 sandwiches</td><td>5 pennies</td><td>7 quarters</td><td>6 sandwiches</td></tr>
</table>

6 apples __________

6 games __________

7 blue balloons __________

4 maple trees __________

5 nickels __________

7 puppies __________

7 turnips __________

2 salads __________

4 apples __________

6 popular trees __________

4 carrots __________

7 crayons __________

6 black balloons __________

4 seashells __________

5 quarters __________

5 pizzas __________

27 pennies __________

27 Pokemon cards __________

18 cantaloupes __________

16 blue balloons __________

14 books __________

21 pine trees __________

24 rulers __________

18 seashells __________

31 dogwood trees __________

31 carrots __________

21 rulers __________

24 seashells __________

16 red balloons __________

7 games __________

17 pears __________

11 books __________

EXERCISE 29	**EXERCISE 30**	**EXERCISE 31**	**EXERCISE 32**
30 pencils	11 dogwood trees	21 seashells	14 watermelons
12 games	37 cantaloupes	16 books	38 pennies
19 books	11 games	11 erasers	4 green balloons
25 dogwood trees	20 apples	17 games	18 games
20 Pokemon cards	17 pennies	31 baseball cards	12 pine trees
22 cantaloupes	34 baseball cards	16 turnips	30 books
11 nickels	25 seashells	18 violet marbles	18 Pokemon cards
10 seashells	23 books	10 plums	25 oranges

EXERCISE 33	EXERCISE 34	EXERCISE 35	EXERCISE 36
15 games	27 blue marbles	8 watermelons	25 dogwood trees
15 books	15 seashells	29 yellow balloons	19 games
19 yellow marbles	26 limes	35 games	25 pencils
31 carrots	26 Pokemon cards	35 pine trees	29 baseball cards
2 Pokemon cards	20 dimes	31 nickels	23 books
3 apples	22 carrots	26 lemons	30 apples
37 seashells	11 oak trees	13 scissors	22 seashells
32 quarters	25 games	21 baseball cards	17 watermelons

EXERCISE 37	EXERCISE 38	EXERCISE 39	EXERCISE 40
28 watermelons	21 watermelons	34 games	24 Pokemon cards
23 plums	20 rulers	32 watermelons	19 books
27 erasers	29 baseball cards	11 dogwood trees	9 oak trees
14 nickels	15 games	17 books	20 nickels
28 Pokemon cards	21 limes	16 apples	20 carrots
20 blue marbles	15 seashells	21 seashells	27 crayons
26 pine trees	21 oak trees	10 rulers	24 black marbles
20 books	22 dimes	15 dimes	11 games

EXERCISE 41	EXERCISE 42	EXERCISE 43	EXERCISE 44
8 seashells	18 books	14 blue marbles	25 seashells
26 pine trees	5 nickels	11 games	28 pears
8 nickels	12 rulers	37 seashells	31 baseball cards
22 games	29 popular trees	13 oak trees	10 violet balloons
16 scissors	15 games	13 turnips	28 books
25 red marbles	17 seashells	20 apples	16 dimes
25 baseball cards	9 cantaloupes	16 quarters	14 dogwood trees
26 limes	34 Pokemon cards	25 Pokemon cards	25 turnips

Visit

BABY PROFESSOR
EDUCATION KIDS

www.BabyProfessorBooks.com

to download Free Baby Professor eBooks
and view our catalog of new and exciting
Children's Books